AF853260

# Augusta National & The Masters

## *A Photographer's Scrapbook*

TO BRUCE
WITH BEST WISHES
Frank Christian


Frank Christian

with Cal Brown


*Foreword by Gene Sarazen*

MASTERS 2000


**SLEEPING BEAR PRESS**
CHELSEA • MICHIGAN

Inquiries regarding prints of photographs contained
in this book should be directed to:
Frank Christian, Historic Golf Prints,
2150 Central Avenue, Augusta, GA 30904

Copyright ©1996 Frank Christian

ALL RIGHTS RESERVED.
*No part of this book may be reproduced in any manner without the express written consent of the publisher, except in the case of brief excerpts in critical reviews and articles. All inquiries should be addressed to:*

**SLEEPING BEAR PRESS**
121 South Main
P.O. Box 20
Chelsea, MI 48118

**SLEEPING BEAR LTD.**
7 Medallion Place
Maidenhead, Berkshire
ENGLAND

*Printed in Canada.*

*10 9 8 7 6 5 4*

*Library of Congress CIP Data on File*
*ISBN 0-886947-11-2*

# Dedication

THIS BOOK IS DEDICATED in grateful appreciation to all the members of my family, past and present, whose talents made it possible. They include my great uncle Montell, my father Frank, my brother Paul, my son Edward, my two beautiful and talented daughters Laura and Amy, and especially my wife Jackie, who has herself, through necessity, become an outstanding golf photographer.

I also wish to thank those who have worked with us through the years, especially Morgan Fitz, Hugh Cross, Philip Merry, Frank Lazenby, Will Tullis, Jeff McBride, Bill Thompson, Rowland Dye, and Barry Koenig.

For their help in verifying facts and obtaining statistics, sincere appreciation goes to Kathryn Murphy of the Augusta National staff, Bill Inglish, Al Ludwick, and Dick Taylor.

And, finally, a special thanks to John Clouse and Nikon for continuing support and technical assistance.

# FOREWORD

AS I WALKED OFF THE FINAL HOLE at the 1935 Masters, Frank Christian, Sr. was there with his camera to record the event. That same year, his son, Frank Christian, Jr., was born. In time, the son succeeded the father as the photographer at the Augusta National. My own career at the Masters has been documented by four generations of the Christian family.

You know, Bob Jones and I were born in the same year, we both married girls named Mary, and we became good friends. I've had a wonderful association with the Augusta National and the Masters. In my lifetime, they have become an important part of American golf, so I was glad that Frank Christian decided to publish this collection of his photographs of the club and the tournament.

Starting with Bob Jones and Cliff Roberts and continuing all the way to Jack Stephens today, the Augusta National Golf Club has done a great deal to preserve golf's traditions. Many of them are pictured in this book. I know you'll enjoy this collection of Frank Christian's photographs.

**Gene Sarazen**
*Marco Island, Florida*
*June, 1996*

# Table of Contents

*Frank Christian*
*The Photographical Historian of*
*The Augusta National Golf Club*
*Clifford Roberts*
*1974*

# INTRODUCTION

IN OCTOBER OF 1860, a group of rather shabby tradesmen gathered at the small village of Prestwick on the Ayrshire coast of Scotland to compete amongst themselves for a silver-studded, red Morocco challenge belt. These tradesmen were greenkeepers and clubmakers, the lowly service minions of golf, having arrived at their stations through menial labor as caddies and apprentices. Though all had attained a practiced skill at the game, of course they were "professionals," not amateurs.

Matches among professionals were fairly common then, none more keenly anticipated than those between Tom Morris, Sr., of St. Andrews and Willie Park, Sr., of Musselburgh. These two were the acknowledged best of their day. Morris was rather broad and stocky, with a game built upon sound strategy and accurate striking. Old Tom was also a man of agreeable but unflappable demeanor. Park was tall and lanky and played with something of a gambling style, but he was a good match player and a brilliant putter. He was the Ben Crenshaw of his day, only better, and, as we know too well, a good putter is a match for any man.

Each center of golf throughout Britain's island kingdom had its champion, and the time had come to stage a golf tournament to determine the best of the lot, or so it seemed to the people of Prestwick Golf Club, who organized the event. They must have been encouraged in this by the fact that Tom Morris, a St. Andrews man, had been lured away from the Auld Grey Toun to take up duties as greenkeeper at Prestwick, and was odds-on favorite to win. There would be eight competitors, seven representing the Scottish clubs at Perth, Musselburgh, Bruntsfield, Prestwick, St. Andrews, and Prestwick St. Nicholas, and one from Blackheath in England, who happened to be a Scotsman.

It was to be three rounds over the twelve-hole Prestwick course in one day. Though this day's competition was not "open" in any sense, the organizers decided that future renewals would, indeed, be open to any challengers in the world, professional or amateur, and thus this small tournament in 1860 became the first Open Championship of Britain. Willie Park won it, with Old Tom not far behind. Each of these men would win four Open Championships and, between them, seven of the first eight. Morris' son, Young Tom, would win four before his sad death at the age of twenty-four, and Park's son, Willie, Jr., would win two.

In their charming little history, *A Century of Opens*, Geoffrey Cousins and Tom Scott described those hard-bitten fellows, clothed in shaggy beards, sea-faring caps, and baggy trousers as genuine pioneers, paving the way for the lords of golf — the Hagens, Palmers, Nicklauses, and their millions — who were to come. Those simple men at Prestwick, they went on, couldn't have imagined what they were starting, and if you had told them of the riches and fame this first professional tournament would lead to, they'd have been too stunned to speak.

The professional game quickly grew in stature until, with the coming of the Great Triumvirate of Vardon, Taylor, and Braid, the professionals were dominating the game. Since that time, possibly two amateurs, John Ball in England and Bobby Jones in America, could be said to have achieved anything like the same stature in the game. How strange and wonderful, then, that one of these amateurs would go on to establish a golf club and a tournament of his own for the successors of those same pioneering professionals, a tournament that would attain the stature of a major championship (and that

*This photograph of Bob Jones, taken by Montell in 1922 during a tournament was the model for a famous painting by David Jones, entitled* **Emperor Jones,** *which commemorates Jones' historic Grand Slam.*

within a short time of its beginnings) at a club whose existence is rooted in the oldest traditions of the game, and whose founder so clearly lived by the game's most endearing virtues of sportsmanship, fellowship, and grace.

In 1930, Robert Tyre "Bobby" Jones, Jr., completed his sweep of the four major championships of golf, winning the Open and Amateur Championships of Great Britain and the United States. Emperor Jones, he was called, for he had conquered everything in golf. He was twenty-eight. It was the first time anyone had achieved this so-called Grand Slam, a feat no one has matched and one that permanently fastened the word "immortal" to his name. It established beyond question what everyone already knew, that Bob Jones was the greatest golfer of his time. He then retired, and went looking for the site that would, coincidentally, become

*Frank Christian, Sr., came to Augusta in 1927 at the age of seventeen to apprentice under his by then famous uncle, Montell, and six years later became the photographer for the newly established Augusta National Golf Club.*

the object of four generations of a single family of photographers and the subject of this scrapbook.

*Frank Christian, and his son, Edward, are the third and fourth generations of the Christian family who have photographed the Augusta National and the Masters.*

Frank Christian, who is the author of this book, is the third generation of his family to photograph the Augusta National Golf Club. His son, Edward, is the fourth. Frank's photographs of the Augusta National and the Masters have appeared all over the world in many books and leading magazines. The Christian family is no ordinary clan of photographers. Frank's father served as the club's photographer at the invitation of its founders, Bob Jones and Clifford Roberts, from just before its inception in 1931 until 1954, at which time Frank assumed his father's duties.

The Christians and their kin have been residents of Augusta, Georgia, since 1897, when Frank's great uncle, Juan Montell, arrived from Sicily to establish a photography business. Adopting "Montell" as his professional

*Juan Montell, who adopted the professional name of Montell when he emigrated from Italy in 1897, established a photography business in Augusta, Georgia, that has continued through four generations.*

name, he photographed the property long before it was converted into a golf club and, indeed, photographed many of the city's visiting golfers, who included Bob Jones, during the 1920s. The Christian family's connection with and dedication to Jones, the man, and the club that became his legacy has lasted nearly seventy-five years.

When Bob Jones began looking for suitable ground to build his golf course and establish a club, he seemed to be following something more than an impulse. He was finished with the rigors of championship golf, and, as few could bring themselves to understand, Jones saw more important pursuits in family and business. Perhaps it was a boyhood dream, perhaps an obsession, but more likely it was a logical expression of his love of the game, much of it acquired in golf's spiritual home, St. Andrews, Scotland.

Like many another, Jones had been less than pleased with the Old Course on his first visit, but had grown to appreciate its merits and, eventually, to love it. The reason, he said, was that there was more to be learned on this course than any other, and Jones, who had earned degrees in mechanical engineering at Georgia Tech and English literature at Harvard, and studied the law at Emory, was an insatiable learner. He also came to admire this course for its call upon a player's patience and resolve, and its impartial, even rather impudent way of dispensing luck. This was entirely to his liking.

*Bob Jones was photographed by Montell in a moment of relaxation in Waynesboro, Georgia, where the young golfer often went to hunt quail. His companion is George Washington Wilson, a regular hunting assistant.*

*Dr. Alister Mackenzie, at left, explores the terrain at the Augusta National site with its founder, Bob Jones, as the two men work out the design of the golf course.*

How much, I wonder, did this affection for the origins of the game influence his choice of Dr. Alister Mackenzie, the Scottish-English medical man and golf architect, as his collaborator on the design of the Augusta National? I suppose we shall never know, but whatever Jones' reasons, they were not romantic. He had clear, tough-minded views of the playing values and intellectual features he wanted for this new golf course, and must have sensed that Mackenzie was the man to help him bring these ideas to life.

Jones, an intellectual himself, wouldn't have scoffed at the notion that golf and golf design are largely mental exercises; indeed, his considerable writings are filled with proofs that they are. Mackenzie would have understood this and would have shown himself to be sympathetic to Jones' ideas. Jones had seen at Cypress Point in California Mackenzie's eye for the artistic line and his instinct for laying a golf hole into the natural landscape without the one intruding upon the other.

Mackenzie, who had been born in Yorkshire of an English mother and Scottish father, had nearly always played to his Scottish heritage and, by this time, had already penned notes and observations to himself about the Old Course at St. Andrews which were later made into a book. During their conversations, Jones had been made aware of Mackenzie's deep regard for the intricacies and mysteries of the Old Course, qualities that Jones himself admired and was keen to reproduce on his own American golf course.

The link between The Old Course and the Augusta National can be drawn, if at all, through the minds of its two designers. This would explain many of the features of the Augusta National course — the humps and hollows, the wide open fairways, the large, rolling greens — that provide a link between two distinctly different settings and, through Jones and Mackenzie, between one golfing era and another. These connections are sensed rather than seen. Years later, casting his eye across the mature Augusta National golf course, writer Herbert Warren Wind admitted: "I still consider Augusta National the most beautiful inland course in the world, and the view from its

*The view from the terrace of the Augusta National clubhouse takes in the broad lawn and the rolling terrain of the golf course as it spreads out in the distance.*

terrace — the majestic sweep of the land rolling all the way from the clubhouse down to Rae's Creek, with the holes set off by tall upland pines rising like Gothic spires — gets into a person's bloodstream as does no other in golf, unless it be the view of the Old Course at St. Andrews from the Royal & Ancient clubhouse."

For many of us, the links with history and tradition are powerful and welcome accompaniments to golf, furnishing us with much of our appreciation, and thus pleasure, for the game. In this category, one would certainly include the visual artifacts, especially historical photographs, those frozen snippets of memory that might otherwise be lost. And, of these, none are more welcome than the collection you hold in your hands.

During preparations for this book, it was necessary to join with Frank Christian in a comprehensive search of his rather extensive storage vaults. At the time, his individual photographs were not catalogued on a computer file, as they now are, and so I cannot guess how many photographs we examined. Between black and white prints, raw negatives, glass plates, and color transparencies, I am quite certain there were tens, perhaps hundreds of thousands. The best of these are here, in this book. At one point, as Frank was sorting though an old wooden crate, he pulled out a glass negative and blew the dust from its surface, revealing Magnolia Lane as it appeared in the 1870s. As has been mentioned, Frank and his family have been shooting and collecting these photographs for nearly a century, and it is probably fair to say that this book contains a goodly share of the important photographs from the first sixty-five years of both the club and the tournament.

People had been calling for these photographs long before Clifford Roberts, the first chairman of the Augusta National and the Masters, began referring to Frank Christian as the photographic historian of the Augusta National. Publishers and writers have been using them in golf histories and magazine articles for the past fifty years. Over time, many friends and acquaintances in golf have encouraged Frank to publish the best of his collection, particularly those that have historic value, and this book is the result. The images are not meant to be a collection of dramatic moments or critical shots, although some may be, but rather the photographic impressions and moods of a classic American sporting event, told in the faces of its people and its landscapes.

*The author, at right, shown with fellow student of golf history, Ben Crenshaw. In 1981, three years before Ben won his first Masters title, these two appeared together in a television commmercial for a camera company, which some people may remember; they pointed cameras at each other, and clicked.*

Some of these photographs have become quite recognizable, like old friends happily met, and some have never been published before. As a matter of course, Frank sought and obtained approval from the Augusta National for this project, a courtesy he has followed throughout his collaboration with the club. The book is arranged in sections, or chapters, that cover the early history and the setting, the beauty of and changes to the golf course, and the Masters Tournament.

Frank Christian not only possesses this rare collection of photos, but he also is a gifted storyteller and, as you will see, this gift is put to good use in the text that accompanies the photographs. When the occasion requires it, he pauses at a picture and tells us the story behind it. In fact, the book might be a treasure alone for his many warm and intimate stories about the club's personalities and incidents from the Masters. Frank has known and worked with all the principal figures responsible for the Augusta National, from Bob Jones and Clifford Roberts down to the present regime. He is intimately acquainted with most of the great players who have participated in the Masters, from Gene Sarazen and Byron Nelson to Jack Nicklaus and Fred Couples. The most important event at the Augusta National, to its members, is the annual Jamboree, a tournament marked by keen competition and warm camaraderie. Not only does Frank photograph the highlights of this event, he also produces an antic film describing each year's festivities.

Anyone who has loved the Masters Tournament, who has admired the Augusta National, who feels a twinge at the coming of springtime because it means another of those barnburner finishes in early April — anyone, in short, who may have taken that famous drive along Magnolia Lane toward the clubhouse, or dreamed of doing so — will probably be glad that the preservation of these photographs and the stories behind them fell into the hands of a fellow like Frank Christian. As well as a chronicler, he has been a careful custodian of one of the richer heritages in golf, and now, with this scrapbook, one in which all of us can the more richly share.

— **Cal Brown**

*These two photographs of Magnolia Lane, the famous approach to the Augusta National clubhouse, were taken more than a century apart. The one above, photographed on a glass plate negative, shows how Magnolia Lane appeared in the 1870s. The color one was taken by Frank Christian in 1992. The Magnolia trees were planted before the Civil War by Dennis Redman, an entrepreneur who converted the 365 acres that became the Augusta National into an indigo plantation.*

*This photo of the great foursome was taken in 1935. Tommy Armour, Walter Hagen and Gene Sarazen watch as Bob Jones tees off on number one. The copy on the top of the page was hand-painted with transparent oils to provide an early "color" photograph.*

# The Setting

WHEN PEOPLE THINK OF THE Augusta National Golf Club, usually they think of its beauty, and when they picture its beauty, invariably they mean its appearance in spring, at Masters time, with its flashes of flowering crabapple and graceful dogwood and blazing streaks of azalea. What attracts us so irresistibly are those glorious patches of color against a majestic green canvas of turf and trees.

One afternoon in the fall, I thought about this as I was walking the golf course searching for a particular setting. To a photographer's eye, at least to this photographer's, there is much to admire about the Augusta National at other times, as well. In autumn, for example, you can find a different palette

OPPOSITE

*The view across the thirteenth green towards the wooded hillside, splashed with dogwood and azalea, is one of the most beautiful in golf.*

of natural beauty along the curving corridors of the tenth and eleventh fairways with their hardwoods flecked with deep purples, reds, and dark yellows of leaves about to drop. These blessings owe everything to history.

When Augusta's civic and business leaders decided to take advantage of the industrial revolution that swept America in the nineteenth century, the future setting for the Augusta National and the Masters was ordained. Augusta, Georgia, had been a center for the cotton exchange, a place where farmers could bring their cotton to be factored and baled and shipped down the Savannah River to the coast. After Eli Whitney demonstrated his new cotton gin in Augusta, the city's leaders decided to build a canal to provide inexpensive power for new textile mills. The big demand was for blue denim fabric for making work clothes, and this required a steady supply of indigo dye.

An entrepreneur named Dennis Redman found 365 acres on a dirt road west of town and started an indigo plantation in 1854. The main building, which was completed in 1857, was the first solid concrete building erected in the South, and perhaps the first in the U.S. However, the enterprise failed, and the property was sold to a Belgian nobelman named Louis Mathieu Edouard Berckmans. Baron Berckmans and his son, Prosper, formed the P. J. A. Berckmans Company in 1858 and began operating the property as Fruitlands Nursery. They grew many varieties of exotic fruit trees, flowering shrubs, and flowers which were shipped all over the United States.

When Prosper Berckmans died in 1910, the nursery ceased operations and eventually was sold to a hotel operator who intended building a resort hotel and playground on the site. However, a hurricane hit the southeastern coast in the late 1920s, which destroyed the developer's oceanside properties and wiped him out financially. The deal for the Fruitlands property was cancelled, although the footings for the resort hotel already had been laid, near the present location of the practice putting green, and were still visible when Bob Jones and Clifford Roberts inspected the property in late 1930 as a possible site for Jones' new golf club.

The main building, whose concrete walls were a foot and a half thick, was used by the Berckmans family as a residence and later would become the Augusta National clubhouse. On the eastern side of the building was a small wooden house the family used as an office. This would be used as a kitchen

by the Augusta National until the end of World War II. A magnificent wisteria vine, planted by the Berckmans family, climbs the back of the clubhouse even today, and is one of its glories. It was the first wisteria, a plant that is native to China, ever brought to the United States. The stately, double row of magnolia trees flanking the entry drive was planted before the Civil War. In addition, a great variety of flowering plants and trees remained, many of them not found elsewhere in the United States.

The buildings are set on a ridge alongside Washington Road, long since paved and now a main artery, and command a wide view of the terrain as it falls toward Rae's Creek in the distance. Although it has been said many times before, it bears repeating that the first time visitors see the Augusta National they are startled at the dramatic contour of the property because, in real life, it is much greater than these photographs or the familiar scenes on television reveal. The drop at the tenth hole, from tee to green, is roughly one hundred feet, to cite but one example.

The early photographic record of the property includes large glass-plate negatives taken by Montell, a well-known professional photographer of the day. Juan Montell, who came to this country from his native Sicily in 1897

*Members of the Berckmans family relax on the veranda of the concrete residence that was later converted into the Augusta National clubhouse.*

*A side view of the building during the period it was used as a residence by the Berckmans family, showing the luxurious plantings.*

and established a photographic studio in Augusta, was my great uncle. In addition to Montell's photographs, which date from the turn of the century, we have a collection of more than one thousand glass-plate negatives taken by the Berckmans family from about the year 1865 forward. Most of these glass plates depict different flowers and fruit trees sold by the Fruitlands Nursery, but some show scenes of the family and the property.

Montell was a small fellow, barely five feet tall, with a big smile and a winning way. His business was centered around the carriage trade. He knew the rich vacationers had money to spend on good times and enjoyed having photographic souvenirs of these occasions. Augusta is at a lower elevation than Atlanta, and consequently has warmer temperatures in winter, which attracted golfers. Montell was one of the first people to take photographs of Bob Jones when he came to Augusta for "winter" golf or when the famous golfer and sportsman slipped over to Waynesboro, just south of Augusta, for bird shooting. Montell's camera also captured early group shots with Jones, his father, Colonel Bob Jones, and friends like fellow southerners Grantland Rice and Ty Cobb.

In the summer of 1927 my father, Frank Christian, Sr., arrived in Augusta at the age of seventeen to apprentice under his uncle, Montell. It was good timing. A new hotel, the Forrest Hills Ricker Resort, with a brand new

Donald Ross golf course, had just opened and many guests from the North flocked to Augusta for the opening. My father knew very little about photography at that time, but was eager to learn. Montell gave him a small box camera, stuffed film in his pockets, and sent him off to the new resort.

Dressed in his best outfit and supplied with plenty of film, my father would make this trip each day to "kidnap" photographs of the resort's guests. Kidnapping is an old term photographers used to describe their technique of "grabbing" photographs of unwary, though usually willing customers. My father would wander around the grounds of the resort looking for likely prospects — two couples playing croquet, a young couple on horseback, swimmers, tennis players, sunbathers, and, of course, golfers. He would pose them in an attractive setting and capture them on film, then rush to the lab and process the film that night. He would make as many prints as he thought he could sell, and would return the following day with his pockets stuffed with fresh film to make new photos, and to sell the prints made the day before. And that is how my father got started, and how he learned photography.

*A "kidnapper," lying in wait for customers of the resort hotels, was Frank Christian, Sr., armed with his trusty four-by-five press camera.*

"One of the nice things about this business," my father said, "is that people love to have their photograph taken." My father believed that his photography allowed him to participate in the great moments in peoples' lives. Sometimes, as a news photographer, he would record their sadness, at other times their happiness; always, their emotions. He knew that emotions are the most poignant and memorable parts of our lives, and he believed that a photographer who documents them becomes part of them. This is a philosophy I grew up with and still embrace today.

During this period, my father came to know most of the local golfers and golf professionals. Bob Jones visited Augusta fairly often to play at the Augusta Country Club and the Forest Hills courses, both designed by Donald Ross. In 1930, the year Jones won the Grand Slam, these two courses hosted the Southeastern Open. Jones won it handily, beating Horton Smith by thirteen strokes. My father covered the event for the Augusta Herald, and it was at this time that he became acquainted with Jones and his friends, who included Clifford Roberts. Not long after that, Jones and Roberts finalized their plans for developing the Augusta National on the old Fruitlands Nursery property.

*Frank Christian, age 6, with the club Bob Jones gave him.*

My father had a bright smile and a very engaging way about him. He had a knack for winning over everyone he met, and Bob Jones was no exception. They got along very well, and became fast friends. Eventually, my father was asked to be the photographer for the club, and accepted. He captured the scene when the first tree was cut in clearing the terrain for the fairways. He also photographed some of the construction of the course and documented the early activities of the members. My father was very active at the club until a massive heart attack forced him to retire in 1954.

My earliest memory of the Augusta National is a happy one. My father often took me with him on errands, as was the case on this occasion in 1941 or 1942. He stopped to see Ed Dudley, the golf pro at the Augusta National, and, while we were there, Bob Jones dropped by and they began to visit. Naturally, my father introduced me. Memories grow hazy with time, but I can still remember Bob Jones' soft voice and mild manner as he spoke to me that day. He handed me a used, wooden-shafted iron club and showed me the proper way to hold it. It was mine, he said.

One lesson, even from Bob Jones, was not enough to start me on the way to a life in golf, but over the next few summers I would carry that old hickory-shafted club with me nearly everywhere. I would try to hit any small object I came upon, including small rocks and old baseballs. Of course, it was not cut down in size, which was kind of awkward for a little guy, but that golf club provided me with the perfect implement for knocking objects along the ground.

When the Augusta National reopened, following World War II, in 1946, I spent a good deal of time following my father around as he covered the events at the club. I began to photograph on my own in 1948 and took many of the on-course photographs during the Masters Tournament while my father was busy shooting the obligatory set-up and publicity shots near the clubhouse. I continued to assist my father until he retired in the fall of 1954. From that time until the present, I have served as the club's photographer, covering the members' events as well as the official functions for the Masters Tournament, though missing a number of years while serving in the U. S. Air Force during the late 1950s and early 1960s.

I think it should be said that this scrapbook of mine is not a history of the Augusta National Golf Club. That history was set down very ably and in

BEFORE THERE WAS GOLF, Rae's Creek was a place for picnics and recreation; this photograph was made around the turn of the century. During World War II, when the Augusta National was closed, my older brother, Toni, and I would gather with our playmates and walk the few blocks from our house to the inviting shores of Rae's Creek, where we had discovered the ideal swimming hole in front of the twelfth green. We would take rocks and dam the creek to create several deep holes within the pond, just perfect for running jumps taken from the high side of the creek.

Like other patriotic citizens who were growing "Victory" gardens to help the war effort, the Augusta National was doing its part by raising cows and turkeys on the golf course. After swimming, a great part of our fun was to throw cow biscuits at one another and chase the cows up and down the fairways. It was a grand place to play, and we thought of it as just a big playground. Years later, I realized what hallowed ground our playground actually was, and the memories of those carefree days of our youth remain precious.

depth by Clifford Roberts in his book, *The Story of the Augusta National Golf Club*. Nor is it a history of the Masters Tournament, which has been well-documented elsewhere, although it does contain photos of many historic moments from the tournament. This book is a collection of my favorite photographs, some never before published, framed by personal recollections of the tournament, and some of the characters and incidents that have made it so memorable. It's a photographic journey through memories of times past, from the earliest days of the Augusta National and the Masters up to the present, capturing what four generations of my family have seen through our lenses.

One more thing should be mentioned. In the chapter about "The Club," many of the stories center around Clifford Roberts, the chairman of the Augusta National and the Masters from 1934 until his death in 1977. There are reasons for this. For one thing, these are among the more entertaining stories that are remembered and continue to circulate around the club. For another, to many people both within the Augusta National and outside it, Cliff Roberts came to personify the club in a way that Bob Jones never did, nor could. Clifford Roberts was a symbol of the Augusta National's conservative soul and its great regard for tradition itself, just as Jones was a symbol of its spirit of sportsmanship and the great traditions of the game. Finally, Mr. Roberts was the first and for so long a time the principal contact for me and my father in our collective role as photographers to the Augusta National, and he influenced our work in so many ways, just as he did the club. It seems natural to me that he would be the focus of many of these stories.

One of the odd things about the Augusta National is that millions of Americans — and now, thanks to television, millions around the world — have something approaching an intimate relationship with the place. They have seen it so often that it is probably the most recognizable golf course in America. While this book may provide readers with a view inside the tournament that outsiders rarely see, I hope the photographs we have chosen will evoke a feeling for this place golfers have come to know so well and where my family and I have spent so much of our lives.

What I hope comes across, too, is the feeling of warmth and fellowship that, to me, have always characterized the Augusta National. Its membership is made up of the kind of people who rise to the occasion, who have

*This scratchboard sketch of Clifford Roberts, wearing a high collar, was copied from a photograph by Montell, taken in the 1920s; Roberts particularly liked it, and asked artist Anthony Ravielli to draw this version.*

*An unusual view of the sixteenth green, taken from the hillside near the sixth tee.*

become leaders of our country and of business, and, yet, who are, for the most part, kind and considerate gentlemen. If the Augusta National has a reputation for dignity and protocol, it is also true, though perhaps less apparent to the public, that the atmosphere within the club is one of easy banter, good humor, and camaraderie.

During those years when I was growing up around the club, whenever Bob Jones saw me he always took time to stop and visit. He was a very gentle person, with a warm, soft, southern accent and a beautiful command of the English language. He would always ask how my father was, how was I doing in school, and how was my golf game progressing? Was I practicing? Was I studying my schoolwork? What I am getting at is that when he talked with me, he gave me his full attention. He was not the kind of person who avoided eye contact. He looked you straight in the eye. You knew he was interested in your answers and had all the time in the world for you.

Jones was that way with everyone, and I think that is one of the reasons people loved him. He was never boastful, nor did I ever hear him say anything about himself or his own golf game. I think his reputation as a gentleman, for his courtesy and sportsmanship, were genuine and came from within the man. It is this innate sense of courtesy and fairness of his, I think, that spreads across the grounds at the Augusta National, and has always had a subtle but pervasive influence on the atmosphere of the club and its setting.

*The Immortal Bobby, at rest and enjoying it, changes shoes beside his locker at the Augusta National.*

*A view, dating from the turn of the century, in front of the Berckmans house, looking back from what is now the east practice range.*

*A member of the Berckmans family views a strange landscape covered with snow, a substance that visits Augusta only rarely.*

# ROUGH AS A COBB

TYRUS RAYMOND "TY" COBB was a friend of Grantland Rice, the famous sportswriter and early member of the Augusta National Golf Club, and a frequent visitor and golfing companion of both Rice and Bob Jones. Ty Cobb had retired from baseball in 1928, one of the game's immortals. He was known as the Georgia Peach, but, as everyone knew at the time, the nickname was a tribute to his talent, not his disposition. He had invested heavily in the Coca Cola Company of Atlanta, and, by 1941, his stock was said to be worth millions. In spite of his wealth, Cobb was not known for his willingness to part with money, nor, as will be seen, for his grasp of English grammar. On the facing page is a letter, dated September 24, 1941, from Cobb to my father, which complains about the charges for a dozen photographs.

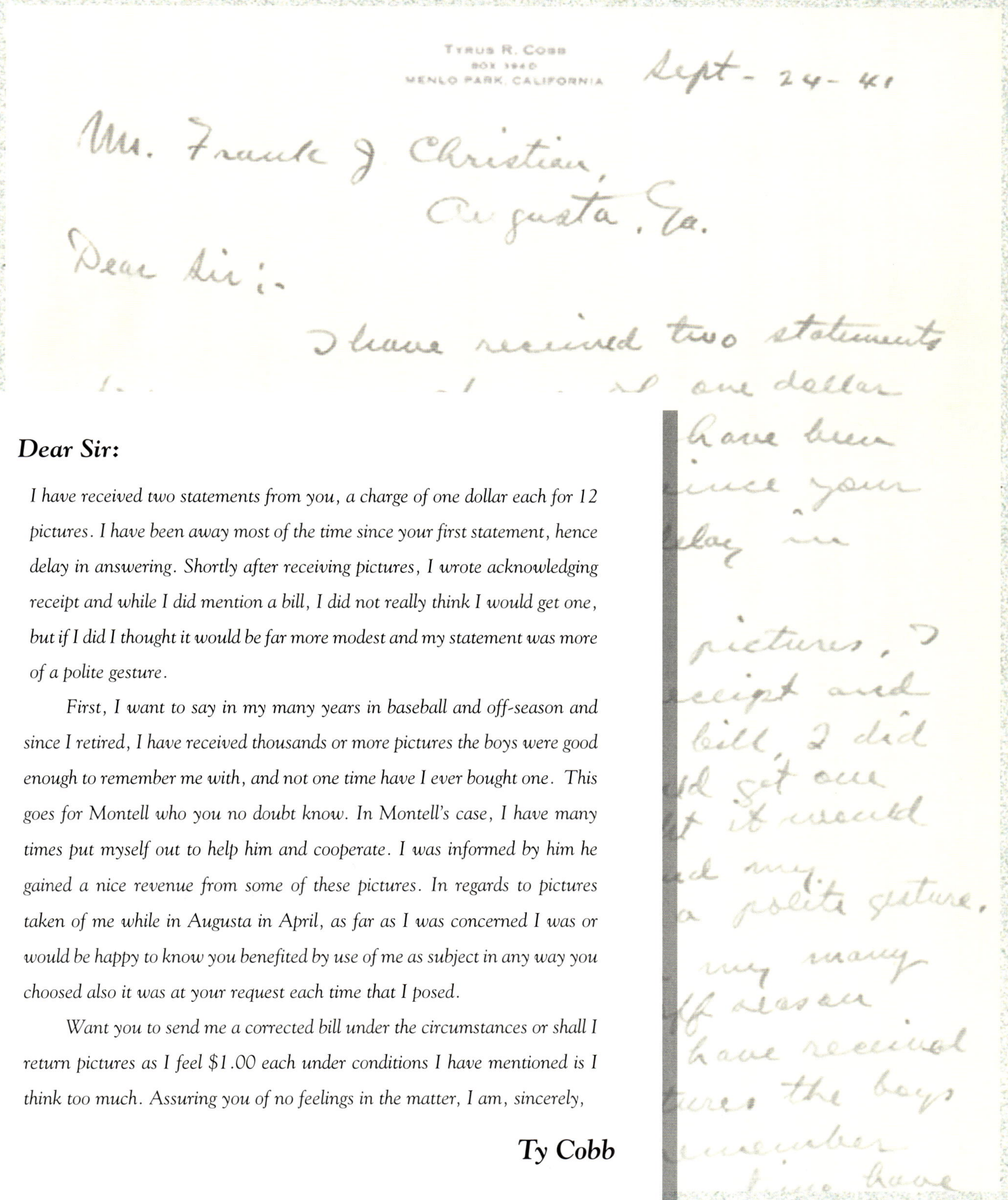

Tyrus R. Cobb
Box 1940
Menlo Park, California

Sept-24-41

Mr. Frank J Christian,
Augusta, Ga.

Dear Sir:-

I have received two statements

**Dear Sir:**

*I have received two statements from you, a charge of one dollar each for 12 pictures. I have been away most of the time since your first statement, hence delay in answering. Shortly after receiving pictures, I wrote acknowledging receipt and while I did mention a bill, I did not really think I would get one, but if I did I thought it would be far more modest and my statement was more of a polite gesture.*

*First, I want to say in my many years in baseball and off-season and since I retired, I have received thousands or more pictures the boys were good enough to remember me with, and not one time have I ever bought one. This goes for Montell who you no doubt know. In Montell's case, I have many times put myself out to help him and cooperate. I was informed by him he gained a nice revenue from some of these pictures. In regards to pictures taken of me while in Augusta in April, as far as I was concerned I was or would be happy to know you benefited by use of me as subject in any way you choosed also it was at your request each time that I posed.*

*Want you to send me a corrected bill under the circumstances or shall I return pictures as I feel $1.00 each under conditions I have mentioned is I think too much. Assuring you of no feelings in the matter, I am, sincerely,*

**Ty Cobb**

Gallery at 1st Tee
of Jones & Adair Vs.
Match
Augusta Country Club Mar. 21 1924

*This photograph was made in March, 1924, by my great uncle, Montell, at the start of an exhibition match held at the Augusta Country Club between Bob Jones, the U.S. Open champion, and his partner, Perry Adair, and the team of Arthur Havers, the reigning British Open champion, and Jimmy Ockenden, the French Open champion. Montell used a circuit camera, equipped with a lens that swung from left to right and produced this extreme, wide-angle view. The technique allowed him to accommodate large crowds of people in a single frame, something of a novelty in those days and one of the ways Montell promoted himself. The featured foursome is, L-R, Adair, Ockenden, Jones, and Havers; the Americans lost the match, 5 and 4. One of the spectators was Walter J. Travis, three times the United States Amateur champion at the turn of the century and, by 1924, the grand old man of American golf. It was in the lockerroom after this match that Jones received a putting lesson from Travis that, Jones said, turned his career around. "It was mainly missing little putts that ruined me up to that point in my career because I wasn't giving them their due importance," Jones later wrote, "and the tips I received that day from Mr. Travis changed me from a terrible putter into a fairly good one."*

*One of the most striking sights in the springtime at the Augusta National is an enormous wisteria vine that climbs up the back of the clubhouse, planted there by the Berckmans. Already creeping toward the second floor balcony in the late nineteenth century in the photo below, it looked like a botanical marvel even then, and today is easily the largest wisteria I have seen.*

A lily pond, installed by the Berckmans twenty-five yards northeast of the clubhouse, no longer exists.

These two photographs taken from a water tower formerly located east of the office building on the Berckmans property, provide a panoramic view of the Fruitlands Nursery grounds that almost resembles an aerial photograph. Some of the principal trees are visible, like the small oak at left of the photo at left which has grown into the very large one that now is so familiar in its place on the right side of the tenth fairway. Beyond the main building (photo at right), stretching toward the tree line on the right, the future first fairway; in the distance (photo at left), Rae's Creek.

LEADERS
THRU 5

# THE COURSE

A GOLF COURSE — any golf course — has several faces, and the Augusta National, to my eye, has many. At dawn, when the light is pink, the golf course yields images that are misty and faint, like a fairy tale. As the color deepens into rose, it becomes more defined, but still more like a vision than reality. I have never really been able to capture on film what the eye sees, even with the use of filters. I cannot explain this, but I think photographers will understand.

As the morning wears on, the golf course feels more alive. The turf grows warm from the sun, the air softens, and the soft grass beneath your feet gives off a sweet, pungent scent. The landscape now comes into sharper focus, and

*OPPOSITE*

*The sixteenth hole is my favorite because it so perfectly suits its surroundings, and because the pond, rather than reflecting, seems almost to gather in the shapes and colors of the seasons.*

the only sounds are those of nature awakening. As birds chirp and squirrels dart and creeks burble to their heart's content, the golfing features begin to take on defined shape and form, and soon the shadows are casting these features in bold relief. For a photographer, this is the best of times.

The early mornings and late afternoons are a photographer's greatest friend, a time when nature's light slants across the terrain at low angles that illuminate the turf like a candle. Trees and foliage come alive and glow before you, while shadows lend texture and dimension to everything within view. A particular scene may not vary by much, yet because of changing light and atmospheric conditions, it is never quite the same. Each moment is different, and when I lift a camera to my eyes, there's always a little thrill in discovering what the lens reveals at that precise instant.

Those are the moments I savor, being alone on the course at dawn or the late afternoon, no one there save the odd gardener kneeling in the distance. The mowers have gone to the sheds, and I watch how the shadows play on the greens and dance across the fairways. Arnold Palmer says he still gets goose bumps riding down Magnolia Lane each year, and I have the same experience when I am out on the golf course alone. Even when playing the Augusta National when the scoreboards are down and the galleries are gone, the excitement is there. On such a day, *New York Times* writer Dave Anderson had the same reaction, and wrote of it later: "The lady was wearing no makeup, and she looked even better without it."

The sheer beauty and topography of the holes is a marvel. In the quiet of an afternoon, walking along a fairway, I would often think back to those earlier days when the golf course was formed and wonder what the texture of the grass and sand and coarse rough must have been like. It would occur to me that this was not the same golf course that Bob Jones and Alister Mackenzie had designed, because it certainly has changed.

Then, I would be struck by another thought. While living in England, I had visited the great gardens created by the famous landscape architect, Lancelot "Capability" Brown, who laid out, among other notable establishments, Blenheim and Kew Gardens. Brown's nickname came from his habit of telling clients that their gardens had excellent "capabilities." I remember being told that, even while designing a garden, he had himself the capability of seeing what it would look like once the trees and other foliage were fully grown and the great lawns carpeted.

Perhaps, I thought, the present Augusta National golf course is the one Jones and Mackenzie had envisioned in 1931 and 1932, and that, like Capability Brown, they somehow knew then what it would look like years hence. Perhaps they had provided space and flexibility for all the changes in grasses, drainage and distances, and had imagined their extraordinary parkland golf course one day looking and playing as it does now. Had they been standing there with me that afternoon, and other afternoons since, they might have gazed at their handiwork and said, "Yes, this is what we had in mind. Well done."

In his book, *The Spirit of St. Andrews*, Alister Mackenzie described the qualifications of a successful golf architect. Among these, he wrote, were that "he should be able to put himself in the position of the best player that ever lived, and at the same time be extremely sympathetic towards the beginner and long handicap player." Is there another American golf course that better expresses this ideal? From the members' tees, the course is very generous with wide fairways and few bunkers. For the very best players, well, we know what happens to them.

*This view of the eighteenth is the player's view of the approach up the hill to the home green. In the old days, when the pros needed three-irons and four-irons to reach this green, this climb to the finish was called "Heartbreak Hill." Today, they barely break a sweat swinging seven and eight irons, and some need only a wedge.*

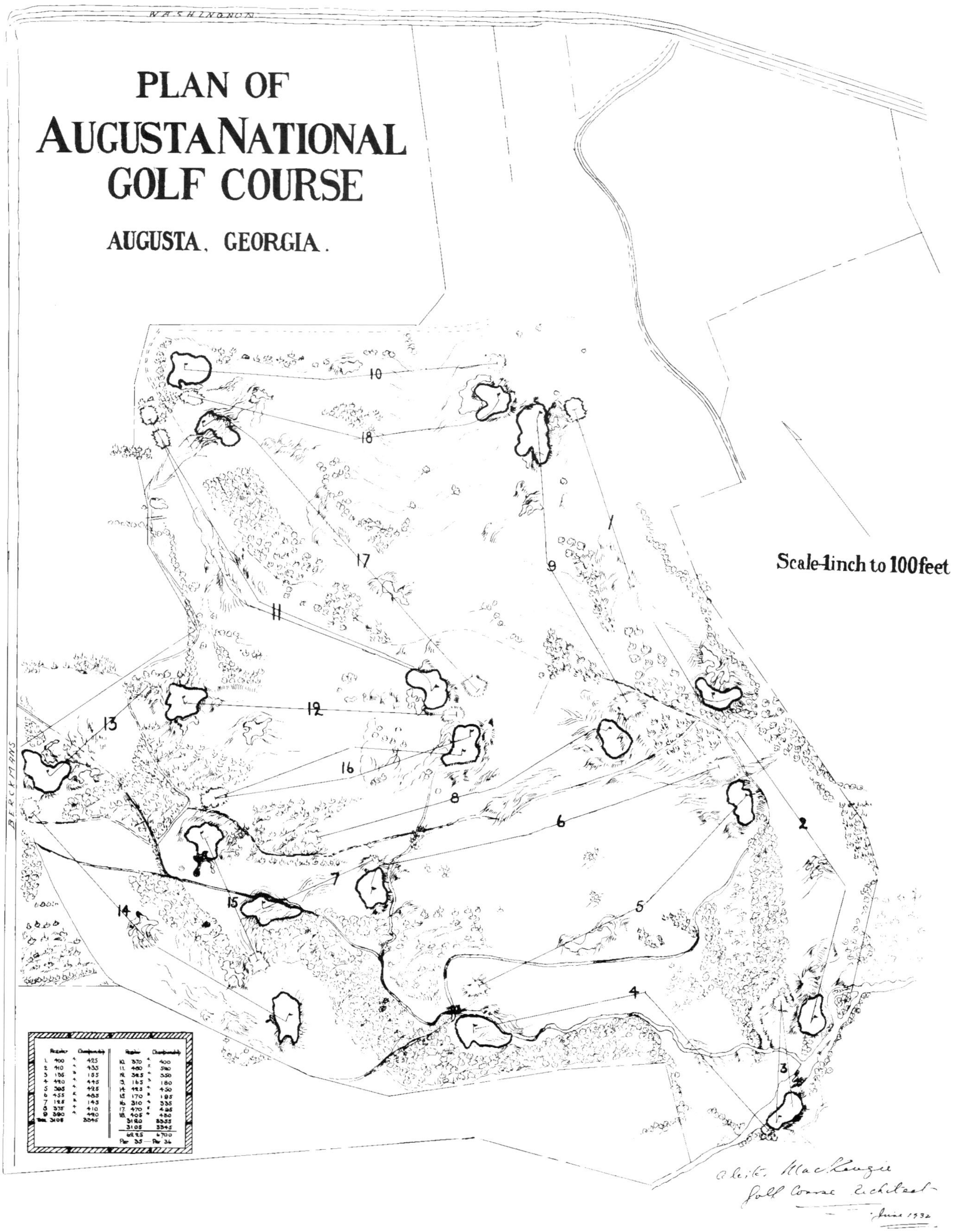
PLAN OF
AUGUSTA NATIONAL
GOLF COURSE
AUGUSTA, GEORGIA.
WASHINGTON
BERCKMANS
Scale 1 inch to 100 feet
Regular Championship
1. 400 4 425
2 410 4 435
3 155 3 155
4 420 4 445
5 395 4 425
6 455 5 485
7 125 3 145
8 375 4 410
9 390 4 420
Total 3108 3345
Regular Championship
10. 370 4 400
11. 480 5 590
12. 325 4 350
13. 165 3 180
14. 425 4 450
15. 170 3 185
16. 310 4 335
17. 470 5 485
18. 405 4 480
3120 3355
3105 3345
6225 6700
Par 35 — Par 36
June 1932

Mackenzie also had a curious notion that bunkers should not be designed as punishment for bad shots. "No bunker should be built unless the architect is convinced that it will make a hole more pleasurable," said Mackenzie, a precept he diligently applied, with Jones' assent, to the design of the Augusta National. The original layout of the course had twenty-nine bunkers — less than two per hole. By 1989, that number had increased to forty-five; today, there are forty-three. They also saw to it that the Augusta National would, in Mackenzie's words, "have no irritating walks from greens to tees and be free from the annoyance of searching for lost balls." This was particularly important to Jones, whose main purpose in building it was to provide an enjoyable golf course for his pals and members.

Years later, a golf fan wrote to Clifford Roberts suggesting rather pointedly that the club ought to make the golf course more difficult for players like Jack Nicklaus, who was tearing it up. Mr. Roberts turned the letter over to Bob Jones, who replied to the fellow, in part: "Our golf course was designed for the enjoyment of our members, who do not delight in playing all day from sand and long grass. For this reason, we expect to keep the course about as it is — meaning in general design and conception — regardless of what the long hitters may do." And that was that, and it will undoubtedly remain that as long as Bob Jones' spirit looks over the Augusta National.

The golf course appears inviting and almost simple, at first glance — wide open, plenty of room, very little rough to worry about, and some of the handsomest surroundings in golf — yet low scores are dearly bought. After holing a seventy-five-footer for eagle at the thirteenth green, which led to a 65 and a coveted green jacket in 1955, Cary Middlecoff thought he had figured it out: "I've finally learned that it's a waiting kind of golf course," he said. "You'll get a chance for birdies if you wait for them, but if you shoot for birds, you can bogey every hole."

The Augusta National golf course has been changed many times since it opened in January, 1933. For one thing, the nines were reversed for the first Masters. The course was finished in late 1932 and opened in January, 1933. Alister Mackenzie, who had gone to live in California, died in January, 1934. Whether or not Jones had discusssed the idea of switching nines with Mackenzie is not known, but after the inaugural, the nines were put back to their original order for the 1935 tournament, and have remained so ever since.

SOME OF THE IMPROVEMENTS instituted by Clifford Roberts were less for architectural reasons than for logistical ones. At the eighth hole, an uphill par-five, Alister Mackenzie had designed a gathering green surrounded by large mounds ranging in height from eight to seventeen feet. It was one of his specialities. To reach the green in two, a player would not only need to play two long, straight shots but also to thread his way past the narrow opening between these tall mounds. It was a fascinating tactical problem, with a bit of camouflage thrown in, another Mackenzie speciality. In 1955, Mr. Roberts had the mounds removed to improve gallery circulation and avoid interference with play; spectators could not easily see the action unless they stood on the mounds, and the mounds were very much in play. Bruce Devlin made double eagle here in 1967, the second in Masters history.

In 1979, the club decided to restore these mounds and return the eighth green to its original Mackenzie shape. Byron Nelson and his design partner, Joe Finger, were engaged to oversee the restoration. Byron's memory for details, even today, is extraordinary, but to be sure of his facts he asked me for photographs of the original green, which were taken by my father in the 1930s. I was happy to comply with this request, and I guess the photographs helped because the restored green is very close to Mackenzie's original.

FAR LEFT

*Bob Jones hits practice shots at the unfinished eighth, watched by his father, Cliff Roberts, and course designer Alister Mackenzie.*

ABOVE

*The second shot to the uphill par-five was perfectly straightforward, but the green was blind to anyone wanting to try for it in two.*

TOP RIGHT

*The long, narrow eighth green lay partially hidden in the trees from below, surrounded by tall mounds that produced a sort of gathering green.*

BOTTOM RIGHT

*The mounds, once shaved to improve visibility, were restored in 1979 as close as could be to their original shape.*

If you compare the two aerial photographs on pages 54—55, you can see evidence of the changes to the golf course since 1934. In 1946, when the course reopened for play after World War II, my father made photographs of every hole. The course was said to be in magnificent condition, and by the standards of the day, it certainly was. As you might expect, though, there is a noticeable difference in the condition of the golf course then and today. Through the years, the Augusta National has constantly improved turf maintenance, just as it has its design features, perhaps as meticulously as any golf course in the world.

Many of the changes to the golf course have been suggested by the players themselves. One who thinks this has been a good thing is Gene Sarazen, who has said: "Augusta National is a great course today, but when I first saw it I thought it was mediocre. A lot of the players agreed with me. Today's players would murder that course. I don't think Jones wanted many changes, but golf courses improve with suggestions from players and architects, and Augusta National is no different. The most obvious changes in the past fifty years are the color and the trees. The course is much greener now because the fairways are watered, and the trees have grown big."

*The ninth green, looking back down the fairway during an early Masters tournament, shows the severity of the slope that so often frustrated an approach in the early days.*

*The front of the ninth green was "improved" in recent years to make it fairer, although the slope is still difficult to judge.*

As the trees have matured, both the appearance and playing strategy of the holes have changed, sometimes significantly. A well-worn story, and one of my favorites, is told about the time Sam Snead took advantage of this rather obvious fact of nature. Never a man to pass up a well-placed needle, Snead was playing in a practice round with, among others, a young player who had a reputation as a long hitter. The Slammer was past his glorious prime, an era when he was reckoned one of the longest drivers ever. When the group arrived at the thirteenth hole, that wonderfully crafted short par-five shaped around a bend in Rae's Creek, Snead paused on the tee to admire the view. Pointing to the dangerous turn in the fairway, Sam drawled: "Y' know, son, when ah was yore age ah'd take it right on over those trees with a little draw, and have nothin' but a little ole ahrn to the green."

The young man needed no further encouragement. He teed his ball a little higher, spread his legs a bit wider, and cracked a career tee shot. The ball soared over the trees on the left and, of course, hit the top branches as it descended, and dropped weakly into the barranca. Sam followed with a nice, safe drive in the fairway, and, as they were striding from the tee, the youngster asked: "Mr. Snead, I heard you were long, but how in the world did you ever hit it over those trees?" Replied Sam, grinning from ear to ear: "When ah was yore age, son, those trees were a whole lot shorter!"

For some reason, Clifford Roberts never liked to use the word "changes" when referring to alterations on the golf course. He preferred the word "improvements." To use Mr. Roberts' term, nearly every hole on the golf course has been "improved." The most dramatic have been those at the tenth, eleventh, and sixteenth holes, and, though less dramatic, significant improvements have occurred at the sixth, seventh, eighth, and ninth. At the tenth, the original green was in the valley to the right of the free-form fairway bunker; it was moved to its present location up the hill and behind the bunker in 1937. The tee has been moved steadily to the rear, alongside the cottages, and the resulting hole is one of the longest, and surely one of the most beautiful par-fours in golf at 485 yards with a drop in elevation of over one hundred feet from tee to green.

In 1950, the eleventh tee was moved deep into the woods left of the tenth green, and Rae's Creek was dammed to create the dangerous pond at the left edge of the green where a sprawling bunker once resided. So

*Many who see the tenth hole for the first time describe it as a cathedral, and you can see why. Because the hole falls one hundred feet from tee to green, it is an unusually long par-four, measuring 485 yards. The free-form shape of the fairway bunker, an Alister Mackenzie speciality, has been meticulously preserved.*

fearsome a hazard was this pond that Ben Hogan began playing away from it, even to the extreme of aiming to the right of the green. Raymond Floyd's dip into the pond during the playoff in 1990, which cost him the title, was not the first such mishap. Many a player has tried for the pin, only to pull the ball slightly and watch it splash into the water. Hogan himself did it during the final round in 1954, the year Billy Joe Patton came so close to becoming the first amateur to win the Masters. Hogan's shot, so uncharacteristic of the man, was played in response to Patton's dramatic charge into the lead; at that moment, Ben had been unaware that Billy Joe had just doublebogeyed the thirteenth. As it was, Hogan would tie with Snead and lose in a playoff.

The sixteenth was originally a short pitch of less than 120 yards across a branch of Rae's Creek the size of a small ditch. It was modelled somewhat after the seventh at Stoke Poges, in England, a hole Alister Mackenzie admired, but this copy was not much of a test, both amateurs and pros agreed. In 1947, golf architect Robert Trent Jones, who was no relation to Bob Jones, redesigned the sixteenth into its present shape. The creek was dammed to create a large pond and the green moved to the right of the water. The tee

*The original sixteenth hole, a short pitch of less than 120 yards, played across this creek bed to the base of the hill below the sixth tee. It was inspired by a hole at Stoke Poges in England that Alister Mackenzie admired, but failed to measure up to the original.*

*The sixteenth was completely renovated in 1947 by golf architect Robert Trent Jones, who moved the green to the other side of the creek and created this large pond, then relocated the tee so that the hole played 170 yards over water. It was an inspired improvement.*

was moved from one side of the fifteenth green to the other, which allowed Trent Jones to lengthen the hole to 170 yards; it has since been extended fifteen to twenty yards. The putting surface falls from right to left, leaving players with many dramatic, breaking putts. It is a beautiful and defining hole, coming as it does so near the end of the tournament.

Who can forget Jack Nicklaus' heroic putt of forty feet up the hill in 1975, a stroke that crushed the life out of Tom Weiskopf. Or, Nicklaus' stupendous birdie in 1986, after his iron from the tee nearly fell in for a one? So many things have happened at this hole. Sometimes, it strikes back. It was here that Byron Nelson found water with his first stroke, re-loaded on the front of the tee and, using a seven-iron, almost knocked his next into the cup. However, the ball hit the flagstick and ricocheted into the pond, turning what might have been a fabulous three into a freakish seven.

You can be on this green and have no idea where to aim. In 1989, one of the game's great putters, Seve Ballesteros, took four putts here, then did it again in 1990. I have seen players aim nearly ninety degrees away from the hole, just hoping to hold the line, and others who look helpless trying to judge speed on the steep hill. This happened to Tom Watson in 1996, when he took five putts to get down: his six iron from the tee left him sixty feet below the hole; his first putt stopped six feet above it; the next returned down the hill again, this time forty feet away. It took three more to find the hole.

On the other hand, the green has yielded to bold strokes. In 1962, Arnold Palmer drove over the green, leaving an awkward chip down the same hill. His companion, Dave Marr, thought he would be lucky to get down in three more. Jimmy Demaret, announcing for CBS at the sixteenth that day, told the audience it was a near-impossible shot, and Palmer overheard him; so, naturally, Arnold chipped it straight into the hole.

The fourth hole is of some interest because it is rarely seen on television and because it was designed to evoke the Eden hole, the long par-three eleventh at the Old Course at St. Andrews, with its famous Strath and Hill bunkers in front. It was a favorite of the Augusta National's two designers, although in his first visit to St. Andrews in 1921, Bob Jones had come to grief at Eden, torn up his card, and withdrawn from the British Open. He had since come to admire it, and while Augusta National's fourth is not at all like the original, one can see the influences. Some of the mounding put in by Alister Mackenzie was softened later on because the balls were not holding the green. At 205 yards, it is a stern test. Only one ace has been recorded here, by Jeff Sluman in 1992. Off to the right of the green is a stand of bamboo and, curiously, a lone palm tree, an apparent holdover from the old nursery and the only one on the course.

The lovely downhill sixth, a par-three, is a favorite place for spectators, who sit on the hillside watching the action while players behind them fire over their heads for the green. Until the 1960s, the outstanding feature of the sixth green was a gigantic mound, some four feet in height, which rose from the right side of the putting surface. Players hated it. "If the pin were behind the mound, you couldn't get near the hole, " said Paul Runyan, a two-time winner of the PGA Championship. "You had to putt away from the hole and hope to sink a twelve-footer coming back to save par."

Jimmy Demaret played "maybe the best shot I ever hit in the Masters" at this green in 1950, the year he won his third green jacket. Demaret was on

*The original green at the sixth, with a creek crossing in front, is seen in the 1940s. A corner of the original sixteenth green can be seen at the right, below the solitary tree.*

*In the mid-fifties, a pond was built in front of the sixth green, but was quickly filled in; the hump in the green is clearly visible here.*

*The sixth green, as it appears now, beautifully groomed, with no creek or pond in front.*

the front of the green, the flagstick in the back, behind the mound. "I had no chance with a putter, so I grabbed my nine-iron and spun the ball into the hill. It was the only way I could hold the ball near the hole, and it stopped a foot away," said the colorful Texan, who was a wizard shotmaker.

In 1991, Jose Maria Olazabal was reckoned a magician around the greens, possessing a touch that ranked with his countryman, Seve Ballesteros. Missing this green to the right, the Spaniard chipped not once but three times; the first two failed to roll far enough up the slope and returned to him, the third went off the other side of the green. Three more from forty-five feet, and he was in with seven, the highest score ever recorded for this hole. Remarkably, Olazabal finished the round in 71, and only lost the Masters by a single stroke, to Welshman Ian Woosnam.

In the original layout, a slender thread of water crossed in front of the sixth green, an extension of the creek that came from the sixteenth. In one of the photographs of the original hole, the old sixteenth green can be seen just to the right of the sixth fairway, behind a tall pine. A small pond was installed in front of the green in 1955, but it added nothing to the hole and was removed in 1959. When amateur Billy Joe Patton aced this hole in the final round of the 1954 Masters, he burst into the lead to set the stage for one of the most exciting finishes in the tournament's history. Fellow competitor Duke Gibson also made a hole-in-one at this hole in 1954; since then, only Charles Coody has duplicated the feat.

One of the persistent pieces of local folklore surrounds the tree which is located about a hundred yards in front of the members' tee at the seventeenth hole. This tree has come to be known as the Eisenhower Tree because the former president had trouble with it. You see, Ike tended to slice his tee shots, and the tree is situated on the left side of the fairway, begging the golfer for a draw. The President was unable to summon this shot at will, and consequently his drives became entangled in the tree's branches more often than he thought was fair. The story goes that Ike complained about the tree, and asked Cliff Roberts to remove it, but Roberts ignored his request.

That tree has grown considerably since President Eisenhower's attempted arboricide. It is a serious obstacle even for a steady golfer who hits a low, straight shot, and a pain in the neck for the weekend golfer who slices. The pros have not had much difficulty in negotiating the tee shot at seventeen

*The Eisenhower Tree, which intrudes from the left side of the seventeenth fairway about one hundred yards in front of the members' tee, is growing taller and wider every year.*

because they hit the ball so high, and most of them play with a draw. Ben Hogan complained of the branches interfering with his controlled fade back in the 1950s, and I believe Mr. Roberts trimmed them in response. But, I wonder if the day is not approaching when that tree will loom too large to be considered a fair hazard.

The club is open from mid-October until the end of May, so there is ample time when the club is closed June through September to make improvements. In 1972, George Fazio was called in to remodel the green setting surrounding the eighteenth hole. The club wanted to create larger spectator mounds between the eighteenth green and tenth tee. A year before, Mr. Roberts had called me in and asked me to make a special photograph of the last group holing out on Sunday at the eighteenth green. He wanted an extra-wide shot, showing all the spectators crowded around the green. I agreed to try, and used a four-by-five view camera to make three separate photographs covering nearly 180 degrees by panning left to right. I carefully pieced these prints together and mounted them in one extremely wide, panoramic photograph.

*A composite print of three negatives, covering nearly 180 degrees at the eighteenth hole, was made so Cliff Roberts could count the crowd.*

When I presented the photograph to Mr. Roberts, he examined it very closely, as was his custom, and pronounced it "excellent." Then, he handed it to me and said: "Now, count all the people in the photograph." I nearly died when I learned what he wanted, but agreed. I made a grid and counted each head in the grid, then moved the grid around the photograph until I had counted every head. I reported the total to Mr. Roberts.

A year went by, and, just before the Masters was to begin, he called me again: "Do you recall the photograph you made a year ago?" he asked. "Yes sir, I do," said I. "Then, make another of this year's final group." So, I re-shot the scene, using the same technique as the previous year, and gave the print to Mr. Roberts. Again, he studied it carefully, and then asked me to count the people. I could not believe it; that is when it dawned on me that he wanted to compare the size of the gallery from one year to the next. Well, I complied with his request, and thought that was the end of it.

But, I was wrong. Another year later, I was summoned to Mr. Roberts' room and found myself in front of a group of members. "Frank, tell the boys about this photograph," Mr. Roberts began, pointing to my most recent panoramic shot, which was framed over the mantlepiece. I explained how the photograph had been shot in three overlapping angles, then pieced together.

"Frank made one of these two years ago, and this one a year ago, and he's going to make another this year, aren't you, Frank?" Mr. Roberts said, chuckling.

Not this time, I said to myself. "The hell you say," I replied. "That's the last one of those you'll see me do," and I left. Later, two of the members who had been present expressed surprise that I had spoken to Mr. Roberts so abruptly. "Well, it was just a private joke," I explained. "That was Mr. Roberts' way of needling me, and he understood my response." He knew I was tired of counting people, and did not mind my saying so. You see, no one could get away with being evasive or untruthful with Mr. Roberts, but he respected a straight answer.

There was a purpose to all this. He was determined to provide the maximum viewing area for the patrons of the Masters. He and George Fazio would go over the ground time and again, discussing where to place the mounds and how they should be shaped. George had his own way of doing things. He might shape a mound a certain way, then grow dissatisfied with it, and shape it again.

At times, he would work at night and uproot irrigation lines by accident. His deadline was approaching and still, to a layman, the area around the eighteenth green looked awful. He had everyone worried, but it finished on time, and it was beautiful. I am quite sure, however, that Mr. Roberts would have called George back and insisted on re-engineering the mounds if the counts on those panoramic photographs had not shown the desired increase in spectators.

For many years, golfers were puzzled and frustrated at the ninth green, which, as you may have observed, slopes severely from back to front. Even the game's best players were left shaking their heads when hitting a shot with a slight draw that landed near the pin, or a few yards above it, because the balls always drew back and rolled off the green. On occasion, you might see one of these players chip the ball from below the green, only to see it, too, roll back again. It took the most exquisite judgement and touch to finish this hole becomingly.

Eventually, when Hord Hardin succeeded William Lane as chairman, the green was improved so that it was more apt to hold a shot. Hardin was a good player himself, had been listening to the pros' comments for years, and obviously agreed that the green could be fairer. It was a popular change, although even today it is a tough green to master.

Through the years, improvements to the golf course have been carried out by many of the leading golf architects, beginning with Perry Maxwell, the gifted creator of Prairie Dunes and Southern Hills, who had collaborated with Alister Mackenzie on several designs, though not the Augusta National. George Cobb, a Georgia native, executed many of the improvements and was the designer of the par-three course. Other architects who have contributed their talents include Robert Trent Jones, George Fazio, Joe Finger, and Tom Fazio. Bob Jones was a great believer in listening to the players, too, in evaluating the golf course. Many of the Masters champions have influenced the evolution of the individual holes, beginning with Horton Smith and Gene Sarazen, continuing with Byron Nelson and Ben Hogan and, more recently, Jack Nicklaus and Raymond Floyd.

For all of its technical nuance and the subtle variations in design detail, and taking into account the steady march of improvements over the years, the Augusta National golf course remains what Bob Jones and Alister Mackenzie always wished it to be, a complement to the site and an expression of its southern parkland beauty. The game it offered, as varied and fascinating as it is, was meant to be a stroll through a well-placed nursery — in short, a walk in the park. And, this quality endures.

The golf course seen in its quiet moments is so very different from its appearance during the Masters. In the Masters, the course is a frame, a canvas, a series of emerald green ribbons between a sea of spectators. The people and the players are the principal actors, the golf course a stage, chopped into scenes. But, away from the Masters and seen by itself, the golf course is both subject and object, a glorious landscape reclining, waiting for the photographer to choose his frame. Its moods beckon and cajole. No human distraction intercedes, which makes for the easiest of subjects and, at times, for the camera, the most difficult of objects.

*An aerial photo from the late 1940s shows the eighteenth fairway, in center, with its original fairway bunker, the tenth tee, at right, in its former position opposite the eighteenth green, and the ditch that formerly ran across the first fairway. The parking lots flanking Magnolia Drive, in upper right above the clubhouse, were long ago converted into practice fields.*

# THE FORMIDABLE FIFTH

THE FIFTH HOLE is a formidable par-four of 450 yards with a long second to a large, undulating, two-level green. The hole is rather plain in appearance, and thus rarely photographed, and almost never appears on television because of its location at the far end of the golf course. But, it is one of the toughest holes at Augusta, and, while players usually are happy to escape it with pars, the fifth has been the scene of unusual scoring feats. Sam Snead once left himself on the lower level of this huge green in two, some fifty feet or so from the hole, which was cut on the upper level. Sam's putt just made the crest of a rise, turned left and fled down the hill, coming to rest sixty-five feet from the cup. He holed the next one for his par. But, on his way to his first Masters victory in 1937, Byron Nelson four-putted this green from twenty feet, and Cary Middlecoff, in 1956, was six feet from the cup after his first putt and took three more to get down over the tricky surface.

In 1974, forty years after the first Masters was played, Art Wall was going along nicely when, reaching the fifth fairway, he launched a four-wood that found the hole for an eagle, the first time this had been done. Since then, Wall's feat has been matched by three others — Scott Hoch in 1983, and both Curtis Strange and Greg Norman in 1987. The fifth hole is seldom birdied, which makes these scores all the more noteworthy. But, Jack Nicklaus topped them all in 1995 when he recorded two eagles on this hole in the same tournament, one in the first round and another in the third, a feat unlikely to be equalled soon.

*The setting at the fifteenth green with its wide pond is a beautiful subject early in the morning when the sun makes the turf glow and shadows play across the fairways.*

# CHANGES TO THE GOLF COURSE

## *1934* TO *1984*

THESE TWO AERIAL PHOTOGRAPHS show some of the changes to the Augusta National golf course over its first fifty years. The photograph at left was taken by my father in 1934, a year after the course opened. A creek is clearly visible running across the bottom of the first fairway in the center of the frame. In the photograph on the next page, made in 1984, the creek is gone, having been removed in the early 1950s. In the 1934 photo, the ninth green (in center, just above clubhouse) can be seen in its original shape, a sort of boomerang wrapped around a sprawling, Mackenzie-style bunker. The modern version, seen in the newer photo,

is very different. Notice also that the practice putting green in front of the clubhouse has shrunk in size, though it remains quite large. The eighteenth hole, whose green is center left in the 1934 photo, also has undergone significant change. The original green, with its long tongue at the front, was shortened and its guardian bunkers enlarged. The center fairway bunker short of the green, seen in the 1934 photo, is gone, replaced by the double-bunker structure at the turn of the dogleg, a feature that is visible in the 1984 photograph. Sharp eyes may also pick out the old seventh green, shaped like a fat "L" and level with the fairway, unmarked by any bunker, near the upper left of the 1934 photo. The green was changed in 1937 after Byron Nelson drove it; the modern green is elevated and virtually surrounded by bunkers. Just to its right, the original second green is seen, shaped from left to right around a single bunker, encouraging a running approach shot; the modern green is guarded in front by two deep bunkers, asking to be carried.

TOP

*The fourth hole is seen as it appeared in the late 1930s, when galleries could walk the fairways behind the players.*

BOTTOM

*Located in the western corner of the golf course, the fourth has changed somewhat since the course opened, but it is still a strong par-three.*

*Originally unblemished by sand and level with the fairway, the seventh green can be seen surrounded by bunkers in the photograph below taken in the 1950s and the contemporary one to the left.*

# AMEN CORNER

THE THREE HOLES AT THE FAR END OF THE COURSE, strung together by the coils of Rae's Creek and the currents of history, have defined many a Masters Tournament. Beginning at the par-four eleventh, with its mulish pond, this triumvirate of holes can raise golfers to the heights, or cast them to perdition. The middle hole, the short twelfth, does not look that scary — not until you play it. The last of the three is a marvelous par-five, perhaps the most marvelous in golf, a tempting and ravenous beauty that has not once in its sixty-odd years lost its fascination or allure.

The eleventh, no longer the patsy it once was, is the entrance into the fateful corner. Originally rather ordinary, with no water, this par-four was transformed in 1950 when the tee was moved back into the woods and the pond scooped out of the very vitals of the green on its left. The slopes of the green and its approaches were shaped to feed into the pond, and now the green was a terror, daring anyone to shoot for the flag. Everyone remembers the dramatic chip by Larry Mize that brought him a playoff win — and well they should — and the two playoffs won on this green by Nick Faldo in 1989 and 1990. Another great moment occurred in 1979, when Fuzzy Zoeller holed an eight-foot birdie putt to win the first sudden-death playoff in Masters history, and doing so in his first Masters appearance. The only player to eagle this hole in the Masters is Jerry Barber, the light-hitting short game wizard, who performed the deed in 1962. No one can recall the exact club he hit, but it must have been a long one, and Barber was a terrific fairway wood player and bold as brass.

The twelfth has claimed its share of victims, none more determined nor more painful to watch than Tom Weiskopf in 1980. Four times a runner-up in this tournament, Tom put five balls into Rae's Creek before reaching the green, where he two-putted for his thirteen, and the next day recorded a

*The pond at eleven is set there to punish the wicked and the foolish. While in contention, Jack Burke once drew a long iron to within a foot of the hole and his partner, Jimmy Demaret, called him "a damn fool." Said Ben Hogan, who habitually aimed right of the target: "If you ever see me on this green, I've missed the shot."*

seven after dunking two more. His thirteen is a record high for this hole. One year, Payne Stewart took nine after hitting his ***second*** shot in the water. Sam Snead played a miracle shot in 1952, when all seemed lost. After driving into the water, he stabbed his third into the thick grass on the far bank, not nearly the manicured dressings of today. Facing a possible triple bogey, Snead holed the difficult pitch to get down in four, and went on to win his second Masters. For sheer improbability, though, nothing is likely to top Fred Couples' experience in 1992. Fred came to this hole on Sunday afternoon leading the tournament. His tee shot landed on the bank above Rae's Creek and just hung there; since the bank has been manicured, no one could remember a ball landing in that spot that did not roll back into the water. Fred, playing quickly, followed this extraordinary bit of luck with a deft chip and a par, which gave him a great push toward his first, but probably not his last, victory here. Twice, in

*The twelfth hole has been called the most demanding par-three in the world by Jack Nicklaus, and others. Lloyd Mangrum called it, "The meanest little par-three in the world." Players are so absorbed in the problems of this hole they sometimes ignore their partners, as happened in 1947 when Ben Hogan was blissfully unaware that his good friend, Claude Harmon, had aced the hole. The trees hovering overhead shade the green much of the time, so in 1981 the club installed a system of water pipes underneath to control soil temperature and allow the turf to thrive.*

1958 and again in 1960, due to wet playing conditions, Arnold Palmer was allowed to lift and drop his ball after his tee shots stopped in bad lies; both times he made threes, and both years he won. And then, there was the extraordinary adventure of Bob Rosburg during one of his first visits to the twelfth. The swirling winds that are such a prominent feature of this hole were blowing strongly that day, and Rosburg was undecided about his club selection. Finally choosing a four-iron, Rossie made solid contact but his ball rode a sudden gust over the green, over the bunkers and the hill behind it, onto the grounds of the Augusta Country Club, which adjoins the Augusta National. He put down another ball, and, with the very same club, stroked this one to within five feet of the cup and made four, for the prettiest cross-country, two-course bogey anyone is likely to see.

For every Jeff Maggert, who in 1994 scored the only double eagle at the thirteenth hole, there are a thousand Billy Joe Pattons and Curtis Stranges. To reach this short par-five in two, a journey of 475 yards, is well within the abilities of most professionals and quite a few amateurs. With today's equipment, it's almost a lock. But, it is just this certainty that Alister Mackenzie and Bob Jones wished to exploit when they fashioned this dogleg around the shallow swales of Rae's Creek. Patton, as everyone who cares about the Masters knows, was leading the tournament in 1954, poised to become the first amateur to win the Masters, but in going for the green in two instead found water, and his subsequent double bogey, combined with another dunking at the fifteenth, dropped him a stroke behind Sam Snead and Ben Hogan, which is where he finished. To his credit, Patton never second-guessed his attempt, saying he would do it again. Many have.

*This view of the thirteenth tee dates from the early 1940s when things were altogether less manicured. The trees, particularly those at the left side of the fairway in this picture, have grown taller and thicker, adding to the gamble.*

TOP

*Flash floods in 1952 inundated Amen Corner, nearly washing out the eleventh (foreground) and twelfth (beyond) greens.*

BOTTOM

*Bobby Locke, the South African putting wizard, putts up the rise at the twelfth green in 1948 while playing partners Jimmy Demaret, at left, and Sam Snead watch.*

In 1985's final round, leading by three strokes, Curtis Strange duplicated Patton's dip into the creek. His subsequent bogey started a slide from which he would not recover, and he finished two behind the winner, Bernhard Langer. At this same hole in 1979, Ed Sneed was five strokes in front on the final day, with two birdie holes in front of him. With a virtual lock on a green coat, and thinking safely, he laid up with his second and made par, a frame of mind that, ironically, may have bred too much caution. He lost all five strokes over the next six holes, bogeying the last three, and tied with Tom Watson and Fuzzy Zoeller. There his bid ended, as Zoeller won the playoff. The highest score recorded at this hole is thirteen, scored by Tommy Nakajima in 1978.

After witnessing adventures like these, the bard of modern American golf, Herbert Warren Wind, had seen

enough. In his report of the 1958 Masters in *Sports Illustrated*, he dubbed this trio of holes "Amen Corner," and never was part of a golf course more aptly named. Amen, brother, to any who pass this way without virtue (and a good measure of patience, as well), and Amen, neighbor, for those who can pass it without blemish. Herb Wind thought this corner of the golf course should have a descriptive name, perhaps not as grand as the Four Horsemen or the Sultan of Swat, but something catchy. The title of an old Dixieland musical number came to him, "Shouting at the Amen Corner." The name fit like a Snead four-iron into a cozy flag, and became a permanent part of the lore of the Augusta National and the Masters.

*The thirteenth hole is the most photographed at the Augusta National, and for good reason. You can shoot it many different ways, and always end up with a beautiful picture. It is truly a photographer's dream.*

# THE GLORY HOLE

THE FIFTEENTH HOLE, where Gene Sarazen and four of the Augusta National members have scored double eagles, invites glory and damnation. Jumbo Ozaki discovered the latter, visiting the water three times on the way to posting an eleven in 1987, the record for this hole, but he did not lose a Masters in the process. Others have. Billy Joe Patton in 1954: splash, lost by one; Curtis Strange in 1985: splash, lost by two; Seve Ballesteros in 1986: big splash, while leading by one, lost by two; Mike Reid in 1989: layup then splash, while leading by two, lost by three; Chip Beck in 1993: no gamble, no splash, no gain: lost by four. The pond, into which so many of these shots vanish, lays across the full width of the fairway below the green. The hole is short enough, at 500 yards for the members and 520 for the pros, to encourage a gamble after a fine drive. There have been heroic shots, other than Sarazen's. In 1947, in the first round, Jimmy Demaret went for the green in two; the ball carried across the pond but hit the far bank and rolled back into the water. Jimmy rolled up his trousers and played a miracle shot from the deep water, landing the ball four feet from the hole; he rammed in the birdie putt, and was on his way to his second Masters jacket. In 1968, Bob Goalby stroked a majestic three-iron to within eight feet of the flag in the final round, setting up a pressure-packed eagle which allowed him to draw even with Roberto deVicenzo, a stroke that led to Goalby's eventual victory.

*In earlier years, the bank in front of the twelfth green was rough and patchy, not the manicured turf of today. Here, Ky Laffoon attempts to blast from the edge of Rae's Creek in the late 1930s; in those days, spectators were permitted to sit on comfortable benches atop the ridge behind the green.*

*How this ball stayed out of the water, clinging to the bank above Rae's Creek at the twelfth, is a divine mystery, and it's owner, Fred Couples, could scarcely believe his luck as he converted potential disaster into a brisk par and went on smartly to win the Masters in 1992.*

TOP

*The tenth green is seen from an unusual angle on the hillside on the right, a place photographers rather enjoy but golfers would do well to avoid.*

*From almost any angle, the sixteenth hole is a thing of beauty. Here it is looking back across the pond from the long green to the tree.*

*The second green, remodelled in the mid-1950s, has one of the wider putting surface at the Augusta National. In 1989, the year he won, Nick Faldo holed a monster here in the third round; after driving into the woods and hacking the ball out backwards with a six-iron, he reached the green in three, then rolled in a putt of one hundred feet from the upper left to the lower right portions of the green. Faldo's long-distance putt erased the previous record of 75-feet, by Cary Middlecoff at the thirteenth hole in 1955, as the longest in Masters history.*

*The tenth green, looking back to front, as Sam Snead saw it in his 1954 playoff with Ben Hogan when Snead flew his second over the green sixty-five feet from the hole, then chipped back down the hill into the cup for birdie, giving Sam a great boost toward his one-stroke victory. But the one we remember best is the putt Ben Crenshaw ran in from seventy feet in 1984's final round, a stroke that started everyone, including Ben, thinking that this was his year. And it was.*

TOP

*Gene Littler drives from the thirteenth tee in 1970, the year he finished in a tie with Billy Casper after four rounds; in the playoff, Casper won by five strokes.*

BOTTOM

*The tee shot at eighteen must contend with the two bunkers seen straight ahead, placed there to curb the power drives of Jack Nicklaus and other big hitters.*

*Among the game's short par fives, the thirteenth hole at the Augusta National ranks very high, indeed, and may very well be, as many claim, the greatest in golf. Rae's Creek, which crosses in front of the tee and winds down the left side, then crosses again in front of the green, sets up the classic decision at this 475-yard hole. Even from so close a distance as two hundred or so yards, a mere toss of iron for today's players, men hesitate before attempting the carry in two.*

TOP

*This view, looking from the clubhouse back toward the Magnolia Lane entry drive, was photographed by Montell, then colorized and made into a postcard.*

BOTTOM

*Another rare postcard of the original tenth hole, made from a photograph Montell took in 1935, shows how the green was situated to the right of the sprawling fairway bunker, a feature that survives today, though in a form slightly altered from Alister Mackenzie's original design.*

*Dangerous and beautiful Amen Corner leads past the eleventh green (foreground) over the Byron Nelson bridge (at left) to the twelfth green beyond, its swirling winds and waters changing the outcome of many a match, and many a Masters.*

# THE CLUB

WHILE IT IS TRUE THAT THE EXISTENCE of the Augusta National Golf Club begins with the man American golfers called Bobby Jones, it is also true that he had a powerful collaborator in Clifford Roberts. If Bob Jones was the heart and soul of the club, Cliff Roberts was, by most everyone's reckoning, its driving force. He was more than an implementer, or a detail man, although he certainly was good at both; in many cases, he was the idea man.

TOP

*Bob Jones and Clifford Roberts, photographed by Montell at the Bon Air Vanderbilt Hotel in Augusta, where they met in the mid-1920s.*

OPPOSITE

*The Augusta National clubhouse at dusk, illuminated from within.*

Certainly, Bob Jones had the name and the contacts needed to establish and build the kind of membership he wanted, but the enterprise needed someone like Cliff Roberts to take care of the fine details and shape the structure of the club. In the end, I think the policies introduced by Mr. Roberts made the Augusta National what it is today.

The reason the club is named the Augusta National Golf Club is that it is a national club, meaning that its members belong to other golf or country clubs around the United States where they live and work. Relatively few are residents of Augusta. Its ranks include captains of American industry, fellows who like to have a good time and who enjoy one another's company. Something else they have in common is a love of golf. They are people who, regardless of their other memberships, cherish the idea of belonging to a golf club.

It was evident from the start that Cliff Roberts was very fond of Bob Jones, and greatly admired his principles. When they met, Mr. Roberts was an investment banker in New York who had, incidentally, fallen in love with golf and who travelled to places like Aiken, South Carolina, and Augusta, Georgia, to play golf with his friends. Clifford Roberts had spent part of his

*Bob Jones, casual but elegant in sportsjacket, chats with Mrs. Eugene Howedd (left) and Mrs. Burma Peabody (right) while seated at an umbrella table off the clubhouse veranda.*

childhood in an orphanage, and Jones was everything Mr. Roberts admired: a gentleman, a wonderful speaker, a true sportsman, and a great golfer. Cliff Roberts obviously had large ambitions, too, and had learned to set very high standards for himself.

Bob Jones certainly set the tone, but it was clear to me that Cliff Roberts ran the Augusta National. He lived on the grounds, and was there much of the time. In the years I knew him, Mr. Roberts was a perfectionist who could never accept doing things by half measures. He had a hand in selecting everything from the china to the napkins to the green jackets. Every small detail had his imprint on it. He never asked, "What will this cost?" He wanted only to know the best way to do it.

In his book, he admits that he might have been a greater financial success on Wall Street if he had chosen to follow that path, but the Augusta National consumed him. Clifford Roberts had been married several times, but had no children. He was very quiet and protective of his personal life, and I have always respected that. At some point in his life, as he admitted in his book, Mr. Roberts had made a choice between his career on Wall Street and the Augusta National, and he chose the latter. He took no financial compensation for his work on behalf of the club, and yet stated in his book: "I was overpaid."

In describing Clifford Roberts, you have to begin with his manner of speech. Although he did not have an impediment, he did hesitate noticeably between words. It seemed as if he were always searching for the right word. He would start a sentence, then mumble "ahh, ahh, ahh," and eventually would pronounce the exact word he was looking for. But, he would not give it voice until he had chosen it. This got to be funny, especially when he phoned early in the mornings. I would answer the telephone, "Hello," and back would come, "ahh, ahh, ahh." I knew who it was, so I would immediately say, "Good morning Mr. Roberts."

This peculiar hesitation affected the way he spoke on television, but he rarely stumbled on air because he chose his words beforehand. Incidentally, he did not shrink from correcting the announcers, when necessary. During one of the early telecasts of the Masters, he and Bob Jones were on camera in the Butler cabin preparing to award the green jacket to the winner. The

*Phil Wahl, longtime general manager of the Augusta National, poses next to the silver replica of the clubhouse that serves as the permanent trophy for the Masters.*

announcer's voice boomed, "And now, from the Augusta National Country Club, we take you to. . . . . ," but Mr. Roberts allowed him to go no further. "This is the Augusta National GOLF Club," Mr. Roberts interrupted, not caring in the least that his words were being carried to millions on television, only that the title be announced correctly. He was a stickler for accuracy, particularly when it came to the Augusta National.

Mr. Roberts was always on the lookout for something that would improve the quality of the food and service at the Augusta National. He was partial to cheesecake, and on one occasion in New York, lunching with a CBS executive at the famous restaurant, 21, he ordered cheesecake for dessert. He found it delightful, and asked for the recipe. The waiter returned and informed him that the cheesecake was Sara Lee's. "I don't give a damn whose it is," said Mr. Roberts, "get in touch with Sara Lee and find out how she makes it. Ahh, ahh, ahh, ask her if she can give me the recipe."

Each year, the Augusta National has a golf outing for members, which is called the Jamboree. It is a light-hearted event planned around a four-ball tournament, and is designed for fun. As far as Mr. Roberts and many of the members were concerned, the Jamboree is a more important event than the

Masters. The first Jamboree was held in Long Island, as a convenience for the majority of members who were active in business in New York, and when the event proved to be popular, it was agreed to move it permanently to the Augusta National. Customarily, it is held two or three weeks prior to the Masters. The members compete in a golf tournament, with partners of their choosing, and the competition between teams is very keen.

The Jamboree was Mr. Roberts' pet project because it provided an opportunity for members to get to know one another better — to let their hair down, so to speak. The members do not really cross paths very often because they lead such busy lives, and he loved to see them come "home" to the Augusta National once a year to revel in the camaraderie and the competition.

The Jamboree, he felt, did more than anything else to foster a sense of fellowship and esprit within the club. Because of this, he was always looking for ways to make it more enjoyable for participants. As a result, he was receptive to my suggestion that we make a movie of the Jamboree.

The idea was to shoot footage of the activities on Thursday and Friday, mix in some entertainment, and show the movie at Saturday night's awards dinner. I had discussed the concept with Phil Wahl, the manager, and had in mind a humorous film using the members as actors to capture the fun of the event. Mr. Roberts liked the idea, and told us to go ahead with it. The first film was shot in black and white, and was pretty crude. I used a few camera tricks, like slowing the film speed so that, when shown at the correct speed, the members resembled characters in a Charlie Chaplin film. Mr. Roberts asked us to produce another the following year, only better, which was typical of his instructions.

In our search for unusual skits, we came up with the idea of dressing Cliff Roberts in a gorilla suit. No one would know who was in the gorilla suit, of course. The "gorilla" was to be filmed dashing across the golf course, causing havoc to players, stealing golf clubs and then vanishing. In one scene, the gorilla appeared calmly in the buffet line at dinner, and in another a gorilla hand reached from under a table to snatch food from startled members.

We made sure that Mr. Roberts was absent whenever we filmed one of these incidents, so that no one would see him and the gorilla at the same time. In fact, Augusta National's fine caddiemaster, Freddy Bennett, had consented to play the gorilla. The final scene showed the gorilla stealing a golf ball and running down a path toward the clubhouse, where he began removing his mask. The film switched to a closeup of the mask coming off, revealing the gorilla as Cliff Roberts. It was a smash hit.

We realized that, as much as the members enjoyed seeing films of themselves, they enjoyed the stunts with Cliff Roberts even more. He was perceived as a stern autocrat whose word was law at the Augusta National. So, naturally, when we showed him in a humorous situation, the members roared with delight. It did not take us long to decide, nor for Mr. Roberts to agree, that in all future films we would include a skit involving Mr. Roberts.

Mr. Roberts loved these skits. We never explained what we were doing, exactly, but he was always willing to be filmed. Phil Wahl and I were constantly searching for new ideas, and I think my favorite was when we persuaded Mr. Roberts to walk on water. It was Phil Wahl's idea from the start. "What if we lowered the water level in the pond at the sixteenth hole and built a wooden platform from the tee out into the pond," he wondered. "Then, refill the pond until it covers the platform by about an inch. What do you think?" Without hesitation, I replied: "Absolutely," and within a short time the platform was completed. We designed it so that a person could walk out onto it directly from the tee, and we painted it dark blue to camouflage the reflection.

The idea was this: the film would show Mr. Roberts playing in the Jamboree, and upon reaching the sixteenth hole he would hit a shot that carried the pond and rolled into the cup. Without pausing, absolutely deadpan, Mr. Roberts would then hand the club to his caddie, walk forward, and appear to be strolling along the top of the water toward the green. When the time came, I went to fetch Mr. Roberts and explained the idea as we drove down the hill in a golf cart to the sixteenth hole. There was a long silence as we rode along on that beautiful spring day, and finally Mr. Roberts said: "Ahh, ahh, Frank, ahh, ahh, doesn't that have some religious connotation?" "Yessir, it does," I replied, "but the premise is that many of the members believe you can walk on water, so we're going to prove it." He kind of chuckled, and mumbled, "Ahh, very well."

I had placed the camera at an angle so that the reflection off the water hid the platform from view, and gave Mr. Roberts the sign to hit a shot. I explained that we would use trick photography to show the ball rolling into the cup, which seemed to satisfy him. But, much to our amazement, he knocked the ball within a few feet of the hole. Then, he handed his club to the caddie and strode purposefully forward onto the hidden platform and started walking across the water. After he took about seven or eight steps, he turned to his caddie, who was hesitating on the bank, and waved him to follow. "C'mon," he called. The camera was still rolling, and I panned to the caddie who was shaking his head. Mr. Roberts called again, more forcefully, and with that, the caddie moved gingerly toward the water's edge.

Well, we had not forewarned the caddie, who apparently did not see the little platform and trudged down the bank into the water, still carrying Mr. Roberts clubs. Mr. Roberts looked down at him in disbelief. What we did not know was that the caddie could not swim, and before we knew it, he was thrashing around in desperation and we were in the water, rescuing him. When the film was screened, we used the Hallelujah Chorus from Handel's

Messiah as background music and dubbed in a sign, painted with little cherubs, that read, "Oh, ye of little faith." It was a huge hit with everybody, including Mr. Roberts.

This was the last skit he appeared in. The following year, he was unwell, and no film was made, and eventually we abandoned the project. Three years later, Mr. Roberts was dead.

In 1937, the PGA of America decided to inaugurate a tournament for its senior members, those club pros over fifty, and needed a prestigious club in the South willing to host the event. Bob Jones, with his close ties to the pros and his customary southern hospitality, offered the Augusta National as host for the first PGA Seniors' Championship. The tournament was held in late November, and Augusta National member Alfred Bourne endowed the winner's trophy. The first winner was Jock Hutchison, and his pal Fred McLeod finished fourth. In 1938, Jones again hosted the tournament, in early December, and this time McLeod won, while Hutchison placed fourth. It was an auspicious beginning for a tournament that is now a major cornerstone of the popular Senior Tour. To find warmer weather, the tournament moved to Florida where Jock Hutchison finished either first, second, or third for the next dozen years.

*William Lane, at right, took over as chairman of the Augusta National and the Masters from Cliff Roberts, left, but served only a short time before his death.*

Cliff Roberts' successor was William Lane, a well-liked native of Tennessee who was now a successful businessman in Houston. Lane had a wonderful sense of humor. He took part in many of the skits during a Jamboree.

When Bill Lane died, the mantle fell to Hord Hardin, a former president of the United States Golf Association. A lawyer and banker from St. Louis, Hardin was a fine amateur golfer who had been around golf a long time. He had a deep love of the game, and was very loyal to the Augusta National. In addition, Hardin had chaired the national championship, the U.S. Open, and was well-qualified to run the Masters. Hardin had a reputation as a witty man, with a keen, dry sense of humor.

In the days of Bermuda greens, which were overseeded with rye grass in winter, players complained about the hard putting surfaces. You could actually hear balls as they rolled across the greens. Hardin pulled no punches about this, telling golf writer Jerry Tarde drily: "You've heard of putting down a marble staircase? That was Augusta." Hardin made a decision to change

*This group photograph of PGA officials with the winner's trophy for the first PGA Senior Championship in 1937 includes the winner, Jock Hutchison, second from the right, and Augusta National founding member, Fielding Wallace, far right.*

the greens from Bermuda to bent in 1980, perhaps his most significant legacy to the course. There were screams, of course, from the players who feared that the new greens would be so slick they would be unplayable. These fears were unfounded, but the change did push up the scores slightly. Since 1974, the winning scores had averaged 276. The first Masters played on bent greens, in 1981, was won by Tom Watson with a score of 280, and for the rest of the decade the winners' scores averaged 281.

*Hord Hardin succeeded William Lane as chairman, and served for a dozen years beginning in 1979.*

During his tenure, Hord Hardin made a number of other improvements to the golf course, including the re-shaping of the ninth green, a persistent nemesis to members and Masters contestants alike. Hardin built a new press facility to house the burgeoning requirements of the international media, which included a state-of-the-art interview area. He also made changes in the clubhouse, remodeling the locker room to add a fireplace and windows that look out on the grounds. Hord Hardin passed away in 1996, following a long illness.

In May 1991, Hardin had stepped aside and Jackson Stephens, an investment banker from Little Rock, Arkansas, became the fourth chairman of the Augusta National. Jack Stephens is known to all as a man of very quiet strength and modesty, and for a sly sense of humor. Stephens is a "solid 11 or 12 handicap," according to former Masters champion Raymond Floyd, a friend and frequent golfing companion.

It was evident from the time he took the helm that Jack Stephens intended to run the Augusta National very much as Clifford Roberts had done. He spends a great deal of time on the property overseeing many of the fine details and improvements, and, like Roberts, too, in arranging things so that everyone among the members has a good time. He has also overseen improvements for the Masters, including a new building in which television sponsors and members can entertain in comfort, and a permanent outdoor pro shop that replaces the old tented facility.

When the Augusta National was founded, it was important to Bob Jones that the club have a top golf pro — not just a star player nor someone who could run a fancy pro shop, but a man who would help the members with their golf swings and with whom they could play golf whenever they wished. To fill this role, Jones considered three men: Ed Dudley, a fellow Georgian; Macdonald Smith, the Carnoustie man who had come so close to winning several Open championships; and Willie Macfarlane, who had beaten Jones in a playoff for the American title in 1925.

The man he chose was Ed Dudley, a soft-spoken gentleman and native of Brunswick, Georgia, who was a fine teacher and a strong player. He had won the Los Angeles and Western Opens, and was chosen three times for Ryder Cup teams. Dudley played in the Masters Tournament during its first decade or so, and always did well. In 1937, he finished third, and in five other years he finished in the top six. He was highly regarded in the profession and very popular wherever he went. Ed Dudley proved to be a huge asset to the club, and, incidentally, served as the president of the PGA of America for seven years.

*Jack Stephens assumed the mantle in 1991, a popular chairman and the fourth in the club's history.*

Dudley had a summer job at the Broadmoor Hotel in Colorado Springs, where he found Gene Stout. Stout was a caddie, and then an assistant to Dudley at the Broadmoor, and, in 1951, Dudley brought him to the Augusta National as an assistant. Ed Dudley served the Augusta National for twenty-four years, and when he left in 1957, Stout inherited the post. Today Bob Kletcke and Dave Spencer share jointly the responsibilities of head professional.

*Bob Kletcke, at left, and Dave Spencer are the current head professionals, a post they share.*

# THE COOKIE MONSTER

While working on Clifford Roberts' book, *The Story of the Augusta National Golf Club*, a group of us met at the club to review final page proofs. Present were Sandy Richardson, the senior editor at Doubleday, the publisher; Ken Bowden, a top writer and editor who handles Jack Nicklaus' literary affairs; Mr. Roberts, and yours truly. After the work was done, Mr. Roberts invited us to join him in another building for a light dinner, and departed in his golf cart. As the three of us were walking to dinner, our conversation turned to Mr. Roberts' extraordinary qualities and his obvious quirks.

"You watch him tonight," I said. "He has a habit of hoarding the cookies during dessert. Tonight, I plan to turn the tables on him." Sure enough, after the meal, Mr. Roberts called for pears and cookies for dessert.

When the platter of cookies was passed around the table, I waited until I thought Mr. Roberts was distracted and quickly stacked five cookies next to my plate. When it came his turn, Mr. Roberts did the same. As the evening wore on, the cookies gradually disappeared. Finally, one remained on the platter.

Mr. Roberts kept staring at it, and finally asked Sandy Richardson if he would care for the remaining cookie. Sandy declined. Next, he asked Ken Bowden if he wanted the cookie, but Ken also declined. Mr. Roberts started to reach for the cookie, but caught himself, looked at me, and asked, "Frank, do you care for that cookie?" I thanked him, and replied: "I don't believe so, Mr. Roberts." He then glared at me: "I guess not, goddammit, since you've got all those cookies hidden behind your plate."

ABOVE

*Champions of golf and champions of business gather at the formation of the Augusta National Golf Club. This early outing included (L-R) seated: Rex Cole, president of the Rex Cole Refrigerator Corp.; M. H. Aylesworth, president of NBC; Robert Tyre Jones Jr.; Kent Cooper, general manager of AP; W. Alton "Pete" Jones, chairman of Cities Service Company; standing: Richard C. Patterson Jr., commissioner of corrections of New York City; John W. Harris of Hegeman-Harris Co., builders of Radio City; Dr. Alister Mackenzie; Grantland Rice; Alfred Severin Bourne, Singer Sewing Machine heir; Fielding Wallace, president of Augusta Country Club and first secretary of the Augusta National, and later USGA president; and a smiling Clifford Roberts.*

RIGHT

*One of Bob Jones' favorite photographs of himself was this one, taken by Montell in 1933. Visible on his watch chain is the gold shamrock he carried as a good luck charm, commemorating his birthday on St. Patrick's Day in 1902.*

# PATCHES

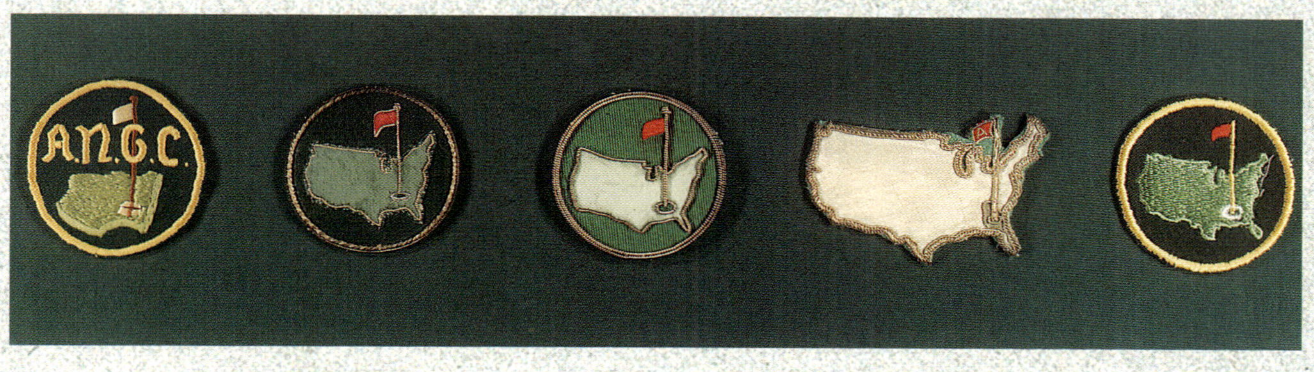


THE AUGUSTA NATIONAL GOLF CLUB emblem is one of the most recognizable in the world. As you might expect, it has gone through an evolution that includes at least five different versions. The first was very crude, according to Cliff Roberts, who explained the evolution to me: "The map of the United States looked as though it came from an ancient drawing," he said. "The members thought it was crude, and someone suggested that the English made nice patches, so I told them to go ahead and design another version. It had a very nice map of the United States, with the flag coming out of Augusta, and it also had beautiful silver and gold silk braid. But, the metallic strands frayed, and we didn't like that, so another attempt was made, but that, too, always seemed to fray. Then, someone had the idea for a completely new design, using the map of the United States without a circle around it. This proved too bulky, so we decided to return to the original soft patch, with a more accurate map." The photo above shows the five patches described by Mr. Roberts. As far as I know, these are the only specimens remaining, and they are part of our permanent collection of golf memorabilia.

*Father and son, Robert P. and Robert T. Jr., at left, prepare to tee off on one of the first rounds at the Augusta National Golf Club. The course opened on Friday, January 13, 1933, and the next day Jones went around in 69.*

*A snowstorm hits Augusta—a rare occasion indeed.*

*Bob Jones was photographed while playing his last round of golf at the Augusta National in the fall of 1948. In the above photo, he drives from the eighth tee, as Cliff Roberts, and Clarence "Schooie" Schoo look on; at right accompanied by a caddie, he plays from the left rough at the tenth hole. The photographer was my father. A month later, Jones underwent an exploratory back operation and within a year he was diagnosed with the disease that gradually took the life from him.*

# THE CLUBHOUSE

ABOVE
*The grill room*

TOP LEFT
*Jones' portrait in the dining room.*

BOTTOM LEFT
*The upstairs library.*

ABOVE

*The Champion's locker room display.*

TOP RIGHT

*Roberts' portrait.*

BOTTOM RIGHT

*The downstairs players' lounge.*

*Before there were real caddies at the Augusta National, golfers recruited bellhops from the Bon Air Hotel, where many of the out-of-town members stayed.*

*President Eisenhower never attended the Masters because of the possible security problems, but showed up on Mondays after the tournament to play with pros he admired. Here, he is joined by Byron Nelson, Ben Hogan, and Cliff Roberts.*

TOP

*Montell made a series of postcards in 1933, to coincide with the opening of the club, and this one showed the former Berckmans residence in its first guise as a clubhouse for the Augusta National.*

BOTTOM

*This view of the clubhouse greets golfers at the end of Magnolia Lane.*

ROBERT TYRE JONES, JR.
1425 C. & S. BANK BLDG.
ATLANTA, GEORGIA

October 8, 1948

General Dwight D. Eisenhower
President
Columbia University
New York City

My dear General:

It is a gross under-statement for me to say merely that I am delighted to learn from Cliff that you have accepted our invitation to become a member of the Augusta National. I cannot think of anyone that I would rather have as a member.

I hope I am going to be given the privilege and pleasure of seeing you there often.

Most sincerely,

Bob

RTJ-j.

Robert T. Jones, Jr.

# A Photo of Ike

DWIGHT EISENHOWER became a member of the Augusta National five years before his election as President of the United States. His sponsor was Clifford Roberts, who also handled Eisenhower's private finances and investments. Ike had been bitten by golf, and had great confidence in Ed Dudley as a teacher. He used the club quite often as a vacation hideaway, to practice his game and to play bridge. Whenever he visited Augusta, it was an occasion. In November, 1954, President Eisenhower paid another of his visits. My father, who also worked as photographer for the *Augusta Herald*, had just suffered a massive heart attack and was in the hospital when I received a call from the newspaper informing me that Ike was coming to town. They wanted me to pinch hit for my father and photograph the President's arrival at the airport.

I was very young and inexperienced in edging my way though crowds, but willing. I grabbed a four-by-five Speed Graphic and a leather case which carried a dozen large film holders with film mounted on each side, and dashed to the airport. To shoot the picture, I would insert the holder in the camera, pull out the opaque slide, click the shutter, and replace the slide, then remove the film holder, turn it over, insert it in the camera again, cock the shutter, fire, remove the slide, and store it in the leather case. I could shoot pretty fast, and had the camera pre-focused and

*Ike greets the press informally on the steps behind Mamie's Cabin. The man second from right, holding a camera, is my father, Frank Christian, Sr.*

# A PHOTO OF IKE
## (CONTINUED)

*During one of his visits, President Eisenhower greets Bob Jones, seated in a golf car that was specially equipped for him; at left is Cliff Roberts.*

ready to go. I'd already shot two photographs by the time Ike emerged from the plane, so I quickly pulled the film holder from the camera, shoved it into the leather case, and grabbed another. I was about to insert it into the camera when a secret service man drew his pistol, and said: "Pull it out slowly." I was shaking with fear. "It's just a film holder," I said sheepishly. He looked me over, and said: "Fine, put it in your camera. Go on about your business."

I had no wish to reach back in my bag, so I walked away. I was embarrassed, and the fact that my dad was not able to be there made me feel worse. I wandered off, and found myself on the wrong side of the street where Eisenhower's black Lincoln limousine was parked. All the photographers were on the other side, holding his attention. As Ike and Mamie were getting into the limo, the President glanced over and saw me standing there. He rolled down the window and said: "Hello, Frank, how's your father doing?" My father had photographed the Eisenhowers many times during their visits to the Augusta National, and Ike remembered me as the kid who tagged along behind. "Mr. President," I gulped, "he's doing fine, but he's still in the hospital." Ike looked at me carefully: "Do you need to get a photograph?" I was filled with relief. "Yes sir, I really do," I replied. So, Ike and Mamie posed at the window, and I got my photograph for the newspaper.

*The entry and gatehouse of the Augusta National, located on busy Washington Road, are portals to an American golfing landmark.*

# THE MASTERS

OVER THE COURSE OF ITS HISTORY, the Masters Tournament has produced more than its share of dramatic finishes, and the drama seems to go on and on. Just consider the happenings of the last decade or so:

- Hometown boy **Larry Mize** chips in at eleven to win a playoff over a shell-shocked Greg Norman.

- **Seve Ballesteros'** red-hot bid for a third Masters title melts in a watery grave at fifteen.

- **Sandy Lyle** lifts a miracle shot out of the fairway bunker at the last to steal the tournament from Mark Calcavecchia and Craig Stadler.

OPPOSITE

*A gallery watches the Par - 3 Tournament, signaling the beginning of another Masters.*

**Jack Nicklaus** storms the back side on Sunday to win his sixth green jacket at age 46.

**Ben Crenshaw** holds on for an emotional victory, his second, the same week his beloved mentor, Harvey Penick, passes away.

**Freddie Couples** receives divine intervention at twelve, and goes on to win in a waltz.

**Nick Faldo** holes a monster putt at eleven in the gathering gloom of a playoff to claim one title, then repeats his performance the following year, at the same hole, to finish off a faltering Raymond Floyd.

Who writes these scripts? How can they top these, we wonder? But, each year they do.

The Masters Tournament has become a major cultural and sporting event that must surpass anything its founders might have imagined. In my lifetime, I have seen the Masters grow from a small, intimate gathering of friends and admirers of Bob Jones, played out in the black and white tones of the post-

*Spectators in the 1930s strolled the fairways rather freely, as they are doing here at the lovely, beckoning tenth.*

Depression thirties, into the richly colorful national treasure of the nineties that millions of people now call their own. The drama, we know, has been there from the beginning, hidden in that golf course which was so artfully contrived by those two conjurers, Jones and Mackenzie.

None of this was known to me, at the time, nor could it have made the slightest difference the first time I set eyes on it. My earliest recollections of the Masters were as a toddler of five or six. The experience was a little overwhelming and, if you will forgive my saying so, a bit over my head. I could not see very much, so I just fell in behind my father as he made his rounds shooting pictures. As I grew older, I began to understand what was going on in this lovely green parkland about me as I learned to help with small chores and errands. Eventually, I became his assistant.

In those days, my father supplied photographs to Acme Photo Service in New York. We hurried to take our shots in the mornings, then developed the film and made prints, which we sent by telephone lines using an electronic drum that transmitted the images. My father would also write cutlines for each photo, and send that information with the image. In the afternoons, we

*Bob Jones driving at the fifteenth before an intimate gathering at an early Masters.*

would concentrate on the leaders, taking their photographs and preparing the prints for transmission that night or early the next morning. Unlike today, we did not spend a lot of time out on the golf course, and action shots were scarce.

The ceremonies and award presentations were the big thing in those days. What impressed me most as a youngster were the Champions' Clinics, when the big stars gathered in front of the spectators and gave exhibitions. It was quite exciting to see the crowds gather in the grandstands and hear the applause as the champions paraded out in their green jackets. There was no television then, so we felt privileged to watch the biggest stars in golf demonstrate their skill. When they staged long driving contests, we were enthralled. It was great fun for me because my father, as the club photographer, was an official part of the festivities. It seemed as though he knew everybody, and everybody knew him, so I became acquainted with most of the players.

These Champions' Clinics were held on Wednesdays, the day before the Masters begins, and, in time, evolved into the par-three tournament of today. The idea of having a special event before the tournament was suggested by Grantland Rice and O. B. Keeler, the two deans of America's golf writing fraternity. At the first Masters in 1934, which was held in March to accommodate the press returning from spring training camps in Florida, many of the golf writers showed up early in the week and had little to write about. Rice and Keeler had asked Bob Jones if they could organize something to entertain "the boys" of the press, who had nothing to do on Wednesday.

Grantland Rice suggested staging an exhibition match between two of the then young lions on the tour and the team of Bob Jones and home pro Ed Dudley. Jones readily agreed to this, and suggested that Rice, who was also a member of the Augusta National, invite Dick Metz, a Kansan whose black wavy hair and handsome features made him a gallery favorite, and Ky Laffoon, a sometimes temperamental but brilliant shotmaker from Zinc, Arkansas, who incidentally went on to win four tournaments that year.

The match was set for Wednesday, and was witnessed by ninety-four people, mostly newspapermen. Metz and Laffoon handed the favored home team a defeat, three up with two to play. It was unexpected, but enormously popular with the press, who were able to file fresh news stories, and with the

*The Champions' Clinics, held for so many years on Wednesdays before the tournament, were as popular as the competition itself, as can be seen by this large and appreciative gallery filling the hillside below the ninth and eighteenth greens.*

*An exhibition match between the home team of Ed Dudley and Bob Jones and young lions Ky Laffoon and Dick Metz was staged prior to the 1934 tournament for the benefit of the press.*

spectators, who had not seen their beloved Bobby Jones in competition for four years.

Both Jones and Roberts were quick to recognize a good thing, and the special event on Wednesdays became a fixture. The following year, it was a clinic featuring the top players, and this evolved into the Champions' Clinic, featuring past winners, along with the long-drive contest I enjoyed so much, and eventually into the par-three tournament.

In the first few Masters, procedures tended to be looser than they are today. They tell this story about Bob Jones' father, Robert P. Jones, who was known to everyone as "Colonel Bob." During the second or third Masters, additional men were needed to officiate, and one of those they asked to help was Colonel Bob. He was assigned a position between the eleventh and twelfth holes. In the third round, rain poured down, creating casual water. A young contestant found his ball near a small puddle, and called for a ruling. Colonel Bob went over, looked down at the lad's predicament, and asked the youngster: "What do you want to do?" The fellow replied: "Well, sir, I'd like to get some relief." Colonel Bob was not sure how to proceed, so he puffed on his pipe for a moment, then asked: "Tell me, son, how do you stand in the tournament?" "I'm eleven over par," the young man informed him. "Hell, you can tee the sonuvabitch up, if you want to," ruled Colonel Bob.

*Long drive contests were held every year from 1934 to 1959, and mighty George Bayer, above, won several, including the last with a clout of 321 yards. In 1954, amateur Billy Joe Patton won the contest with a blast of 338 yards, then nearly won the Masters, too.*

My first experience shooting pictures at the Masters occured in 1948 when I was a teenager. My father must have felt it was time I began earning my keep, handed me a camera, and sent me out on the golf course. I received no pay, but continued to assist him for several years. The first time I earned money for shooting pictures at the Masters was in 1955. My father had received a 35 millimeter Kodak camera called a Pony 35, and I was anxious to experiment with shooting in color. My father had little use for color and did not think much of this "miniature" camera either, but since Kodak had sent us several rolls of Kodachrome film, said, "You might as well go try it."

# THE 1935 FIELD

*This photograph of the 1935 Masters field, taken by my father, was later doctored and circulated with the false label, "Inaugural Masters, April 1934." The players are (L-R) front row: Jim Foulis, Tony Manero, Bobby Cruickshank, Gene Sarazen, Charlie Yates, Paul Runyan, Bobby Jones, Olin Dutra, Johnny Farrell, Willie Macfarlane, Jimmy Thomson, Harry Cooper, Johnny Revolta, Henry Picard. Second row: Andy Kay, Tommy Armour, Jules Huot, Bill Schwartz, Wild Bill Mehlhorn, Freddie McLeod, Jock Hutchison, Frank Walsh, Craig Wood, Ray Mangrum, Clarence Clark, Jimmy Hines, Mike Turnesa, Joe Turnesa, Vic Ghezzi, Abe Espinosa, Walter Kozak, Pat Tiso. Third row (standing): Phil Perkins, George Jacobus, Byron Nelson, Al Espinosa, Jug McSpaden, Denny Shute, Freddie Haas, Jr., Al Watrous, Gene Kunes, Dick Metz, Willie Klein, Johnny Dawson, Jack Munger, Wilford Werle, Gus Moreland, Ky Laffoon, Ralph Stonehouse.*

BEFORE THE SECOND MASTERS BEGAN, in 1935, Clifford Roberts asked my father to photograph the entire field as a memento of the occasion. The players posed on the lawn in front of the clubhouse. I will let you in on a little secret about that photograph which is shown at the left. Copies have been widely circulated and incorrectly identified as the "Inaugural Masters 1934 (see photo below)." The reason we know this is that Gene Sarazen, and many others who did not enter the tournament in 1934, are clearly evident and identified in the photograph. Sarazen had committed for an exhibition and could not play in 1934 and others shown, but not present in 1934 were Jock Hutchison, Byron Nelson, Fred Haas, Jr., Jimmy Thomson, Olin Dutra, Lawson Little, and Tommy Armour. The final indignity is that the print is doctored. The figures of Walter Hagen, Horton Smith, and Leo Diegel do not appear on the original negative because they did not show up for the photo session; they were later dubbed into the back row of the print, as was Errie Ball, who was actually present in 1934, but not in 1935 when the photo was made.

*In the doctored photograph, the figures of Walter Hagen and Horton Smith were pasted in at the upper left (back row), while an image of Errie Ball was inserted between Al Espinosa and Jug McSpaden, and one of Leo Diegel was inserted between Al Watrous and Gene Kunes.*

*Davis Love, Jr. poses above, then prepares to drive from the eighth tee, photographed by the author in 1955; his son, Davis III, below, played in his first Masters in 1988, and finished second in 1995.*

As I started out that morning, a gentleman introduced himself as Davis Love and asked if I would take pictures of his son, an amateur playing in the Masters for the first time. I agreed to walk with him for several holes, and shot two rolls of film of his son, Davis Love, Jr. When the film ran out, I rewound the rolls, handed them to the man, and started to walk away. The film had cost me nothing, and, since he was going to pay for processing the film, I figured I had just done him a good turn. "Just a minute, son," said Mr. Love, handing me a hundred dollar bill, and thanking me. Well, that floored me.

Davis Love, Jr., the fellow I had photographed, was a fine golfer. He had reached the quarterfinals of the U.S. Amateur in 1954, which earned him a spot in the Masters in 1955. Ten years later, as a professional, Davis Love, Jr., shared the first round lead with Arnold Palmer, after both fired rounds of 69. He made the cut, finished the tournament, and returned home Sunday night, April 12, 1964. The next morning, at 8 a.m., a son was born to Davis Jr. and his wife, Penta, at the Charlotte, North Carolina, hospital.

Years later, when I became acquainted with Davis Jr., he remembered those slides I took in 1955 and told me that his father cherished them. By that time, he had become one of America's finest teachers and a headliner in the Golf Digest Schools. Then, tragically, an airplane crash took his life in 1988. Davis Jr., had been a student and close friend of Harvey Penick's, whose *Little Red Book* became the best-selling golf instruction book in history. Harvey's pupils also included Ben Crenshaw and Tom Kite, and, as everyone who cares about these things knows, Crenshaw won his very emotional second Masters title in 1995, the week Harvey died at the age of ninety.

Coincidentally, Davis Love III, the same youngster who had been born to Davis, Jr. and his wife, Penta, that Monday morning after the 1964 Masters, was another of Harvey Penick's pupils. One Sunday afternoon I had been asked to go up to the old Forrest Ricker course to photograph the winners of a collegiate golf tournament, and one of them was a tall, lanky youngster named Davis Love III. I introduced myself, and told him the story of that Masters of so long ago, and of photographing his father at the request of his grandfather. He remembered seeing one of the photographs on the family's mantle while he was growing up, and his mother, Penta, has graciously allowed us to reproduce it here. I had now been introduced to three generations of Davis Loves, and will remember that name fondly for many reasons, not least because it was the first time I ever made money as a golf photographer.

By the time I began covering the Masters by myself, after my father's heart attack, I felt a heavy responsibility to measure up to his standards. People were calling from magazines, book publishers, and newspapers, all wanting special photographs, and, although I had covered the tournament with my father for a number of years, now it all fell on my shoulders. Someone would demand a photograph of Ben Hogan posing with such and such, or Sam Snead with so and so. "Good heavens," I worried, "How can I get these golfers to do everything the newspapers and publishers are asking for?" So, I made lists of everything they wanted and tried to answer each request as best I could. With some relief, I found the players sympathetic to my requests. They knew my father was ill, and that I was trying my best to fill in for him, so they all cooperated.

Players like Sam Snead and Lloyd Mangrum, who had reputations as gruff men, were as nice as could be. Once the players became used to me and I had grown comfortable in their presence, I began to wander the golf course and watch them play. Mangrum was a perennial favorite to win, although he never did, but I loved to watch him. He hit one of the greatest shots I have ever seen in competition. He had pushed his drive into the woods at the long, uphill eighth hole and I happened to be standing nearby. Mangrum studied the shot, his eyes flashing between the trees toward the green, and then chose a long iron.

There was no doubt in my mind that he knew exactly what he was doing. With no more than three feet of clearance between two pines, he launched the ball between them and watched it draw back to the green and roll onto the putting surface. It was spectacular. Mangrum tossed his club to the caddie, stuck a cigarette in his mouth, and cooly strolled out of the forest as though nothing unusual had happened. (Years later, Billy Casper played a similar recovery shot from the trees in a playoff with Gene Littler. The stroke helped boost him to victory and earn Billy his Masters jacket.)

At one time, it was quite easy to obtain tickets for the Masters. In fact, the Augusta National was practically giving them away. I can remember when series tickets were about five dollars apiece and people were going around

trying to sell five or ten at a time to Augusta merchants. This seems almost inconceivable to us today, when a Masters badge is the hottest ticket in American sport, but the tournament struggled for the first decade. The presence of Bob Jones was special, but even that was not enough to bring instant success. Help came from many sources, including local ones.

Almost from the beginning, the people of Augusta played an important role in developing the Masters. They staged parades, purchased blocks of tickets, and generally did everything they could to promote and support the tournament. Listening to him talk over the years, I had the distinct impression that Clifford Roberts understood very well the need for cooperation between the club and the people of Augusta, and he honored this relationship. He felt that the Augusta National should not be an ivory tower inside Augusta, and I believe that Jack Stephens, the current chairman, feels the same way and has done much to preserve this relationship.

One of the things that sets the Masters apart from other major tournaments is that it is played on the same golf course every year. Another is that it is run by a golf club, not an association. Partly because of Bobby Jones, there is a strong feeling for the traditions of golf at the Augusta National, and a lot of what goes on at the Masters has to do with these traditions. It has been no secret over the years that some of the pros have felt, on occasion, that the bows to tradition are overdone and have grumbled privately about the number of ceremonies during Masters week. I have noticed, though, that this sort of grumbling tends to diminish as they grow older. Since its inception, the Masters has been at pains to include everyone in its ceremonies, amateurs and professionals alike, as well as the old timers. Former Masters champions all are invited to compete, and are paid like other contestants.

An example of the bows to tradition is the Masters' institution of the honorary starters, which began in 1963 with Jock Hutchison, winner of the PGA Championship in 1922, and Freddie MacLeod, winner of the U.S. Open in 1908. The two native Scots, McLeod of North Berwick and Hutchison of St. Andrews, were then the oldest surviving winners of our two national championships, and the oldest surviving links to the Scottish "invasion" of American golf. In addition, Jones had ties to the two old warriors. At age nineteen, the young Bobby Jones had been paired with Hutchison the first time he competed at the Old Course in St. Andrews in the 1921 British Open, and three years earlier, McLeod had played an exhibition match for war relief with the sixteen-year-old Jones. McLeod lost by two strokes, and was very complimentary of Jones.

Jock and Freddie were paired together in the Masters in 1935, the first year Jock was invited, and continued to be partnered whenever they played the tournament. Since the late 1950s, because of their ages and historical ties, they had been assigned a sort of informal role as the opening twosome each year, although they stopped turning in their cards in 1958. They soon gained a reputation for fast play. "Everyone wondered how we could play so fast," Hutchison once admitted, with a twinkle in his eye. "But, we fooled 'em. We'd play the first six holes, then cut over to the sixteenth tee and play in." Added McLeod: "We were first off, so nobody was there to catch us."

Instead of quietly easing these two venerable figures to the sidelines, they were made a formal part of the opening day's ceremonies in 1963, and they continued in these roles until 1972, the last time the two played together. In 1973, Jock's bad hip finally gave out. As always, it was my duty to record the start on film. As I was leaving the clubhouse, I saw Jock sitting there on the veranda and reminded him that we were wanted on the first tee. He was near tears, saying he did not think he could do it.

*Jock Hutchison and Fred McLeod, two of the last surviving links with Scotland's gift to American golf, first were paired in the 1935 Masters and were informally given status as honorary starters in the 1950s, then formally named in 1963.*

*Thirty-six years later, Jock and Freddie prepare to start the 1971 Masters; the contestant numbers on the signs are their ages.*

When I informed Mr. Roberts of the situation, he ordered a cart be sent to fetch Jock from the clubhouse, which was done, and we got our photographs. Jock apologized to the spectators, explaining that he could not swing a club. After Freddie hit his drive, the gallery applauded and he walked slowly off the tee by himself. It was the end of an era. Fred McLeod carried on alone three more years, until his death in May, 1976, at age ninety-four. A little more than a year later, in September, 1977, Jock Hutchison joined him. He was ninety-three.

The Augusta National chose Gene Sarazen and Byron Nelson to succeed Jock and Freddie as honorary starters. Neither of these great players had been active for some time, though both had played important roles in the history of the Masters. Sam Snead, Nelson's perfect contemporary, remained active longer, but when he finally chose to end his string of forty-four consecutive Masters, Snead, too, was named an honorary starter, beginning in 1984. Anyone who is present for these ceremonies on the opening morning of each Masters Tournament will understand how much they mean to the patrons and fans who gather to watch and why traditions like these endure.

*Named to succeed Jock and Freddie as honorary starters were, L-R, Byron Nelson, Gene Sarazen, and Sam Snead, a pretty fair country threesome, welcomed to the first tee in 1988 by then chairman Hord Hardin.*

Gene Sarazen was a natural choice because of his historic double eagle at the fifteenth hole in the 1935 event, a stroke that led to a dramatic victory over Craig Wood and helped put the Augusta National, and its tournament, on the golfing map. This single stroke electrified the golf world and brought the Augusta National into American living rooms long before television, or, for that matter, radio did. The radio networks carried reports from Augusta, but real coverage didn't start until the 1940s, and television did not begin until 1957.

The tournament was not yet called the Masters because, when that name was proposed by some members of the press and the club, Bob Jones thought it sounded pretentious, and vetoed the idea. So, the first event in 1934 was called the Augusta National Invitational, and Jones continued to oppose changing the name for several years. In 1938, he finally relented, and the "Masters" name was permanently, and officially, adopted. During those years, Sarazen became a kind of talisman for the tournament, embellishing the already glittering aura cast by the American public's beloved Bobby Jones.

In the tournament's early days, there was no limit to the number of golf clubs a player could carry. As a result, some of the golf bags were pretty hefty. Gene Sarazen recalled that carrying twenty clubs was not unusual until the fourteen-club rule was adopted in 1938. Sarazen himself typically carried only half a dozen clubs in his bag. Most people have forgotten that Sarazen had to go thirty-six holes in the playoff with Craig Wood before he could claim the 1935 Masters title.

"There were no green jackets in those days, and the winner's prize money was fifteen hundred dollars," Sarazen has recalled. "When I won, Cliff Roberts handed me an extra fifty dollars for the playoff. In those days, pro golfers didn't get rich. That's one reason things have changed. Everything about the professional game then was much looser — faster play, more horseplay, and partying. One year, Sam Snead teed it up barefooted for a practice round and shot a fine score. I wasn't too happy with the stunt, and said so, but that's the way it was."

This was borne out by my father, who used to stage gag shots that were designed to drum up publicity for the Masters. He posed Ben Hogan with golf balls spelling out 139, his target score, and Sam Snead balancing golf balls in a stack. Anything to grab the attention of a jaded newspaper editor. Once, to sell tickets, he staged a shot with Gene Sarazen, Craig Wood, and Horton Smith all decked out in football helmets.

The Masters used to attract genuine characters. Titanic Thompson, the notorious gambler, used to sidle up to me and ask for inside information, such

*One of the earliest known photographs of the caddies, vintage 1935, at the relatively new Augusta National Golf Club. Note the number of clubs in the bag on the left*

*Publicity shots like this one helped put the Masters on the map. Here, Gene Sarazen, over the football and clenching a cigar, lines up with, L-R, Ed Dudley, Macdonald Smith, Johnny Revolta, with cigarette, and Horton Smith, at right.*

as the number of people who could be accommodated in the dining room. He always wanted to have an edge before betting. Man Mountain Dean, a famous hillbilly wrestler, would show up in overalls and Dogpatch shoes. He was known as a sort of nature boy, and sometimes he would arrive in a cart pulled by six goats and ask to see his hero, Sam Snead. Tennessee Ernie Ford was another visitor, part hillbilly and part radio and television star, and movie stars like Bing Crosby and Fred Astaire, both avid golfers, brought glamour to the Masters.

Byron Nelson came to the honorary starter's role by a different route. Byron won two Masters, in 1937 and 1942. In the second of these, he defeated Ben Hogan in an eighteen-hole playoff that many Masters watchers have said is the greatest in Masters history. Hogan took a three-shot lead after five holes of the playoff, and played the next eleven holes in one under par, and still he lost. Over that stretch, Nelson was invincible, picking up

*In town for the Masters, Fred Astaire, himself a keen golfer, visits with the host, Bob Jones.*

five strokes on Hogan and eventually winning by one, 69 to 70. Five years later, as everyone knows who follows golf, Byron retired from active competition at the age of 35. He continued to play in a few selected events, however, and the Masters was one of these.

*The sensational amateur, Ken Venturi, holds forth with the press after setting the course on fire for two rounds and leading the 1956 Masters at the halfway point.*

Each year, it had been the custom that Bob Jones would be paired in the final round with the tournament leader. It was a typical gesture, partly good old southern hospitality by a genial host, partly an honor for the fellow who played well enough to lead after three rounds. When Jones' illness no longer allowed him to fulfill this ceremonial role, Byron Nelson was named to replace him. Among the pros, Nelson's reputation as a gentleman and sportsman matched Jones' own, and, in addition, Nelson had just completed a record-shattering year that rivaled the famous Grand Slam by Jones in 1930. In every way, he was a worthy successor, so, beginning in 1946, Nelson played with the tournament leader in Sunday's final round.

This continued for a decade until 1956, when the third round leader was a hot newcomer named Ken Venturi, an amateur who was also a pupil of Byron Nelson. Bob Jones and Cliff Roberts concluded that, in fairness to the rest of the field, Venturi should not be paired with his coach, Nelson, and they paired him instead with Sam Snead. After Venturi skied to an 80, losing to Jackie Burke's steady 71, stories were written suggesting that Snead was to blame because he gave Venturi the silent treatment. Both Venturi and Snead denied this, and I believe them, but it has become part of Masters lore nevertheless.

Ken Venturi's 80 on that final day was not that bad a performance. Foul weather made playing conditions extremely difficult. Third place finisher Cary Middlecoff shot a closing 77, and several others, including Mike Souchak and Julius Boros, with rounds of 80, and a young Arnold Palmer, with 79, struggled in the near gale force winds. Only two men could break par — Sam Snead, a master wind player, and Jack Burke, who grew up in the winds of East Texas. Their matching 71s were the low rounds of the day. As it was, the amateur, Ken Venturi, still led the tournament until he reached the seventeenth, where he bogied and Burke birdied.

In a curious twist of history, Venturi would serve briefly as an honorary starter in 1983. This little-remembered bit of Masters trivia occured because Byron Nelson was ailing and, at the last minute, Ken was asked to fill in. By this time, Venturi was a co-anchor of the CBS telecast of the Masters and, although he had played in a few senior tournaments, had pretty much given up competitive golf. Paired with Gene Sarazen on that Thursday morning in 1983, though, Venturi turned back the clock a quarter-century and matched par for nine holes, stirring memories of his near-victories in 1956 and 1960.

*Three decades later, Ken Venturi takes a breather from his duties as the lead color commentator for CBS, and later the co-anchor for the Masters telecasts.*

Among my earliest recollections of the Masters is trailing along behind my father as he followed Sam Snead and Ben Hogan, the two great rivals of the late 1940s and early 1950s. In those days, it seemed that Snead was always in the lead, always charging, always doing something spectacular, so we have many photographs of "The Slammer." Hogan was the man most responsible for the club's policy on cameras, which did not allow spectators to carry cameras on club grounds during the tournament, nor did it permit photographers with credentials inside the ropes.

I think Hogan understood the importance of photographs in promoting the tournament and the players, himself included, but

*This group photo, made by my father in 1949, was signed by all the Masters contestants and sent to Ben Hogan recuperating in the hospital from the terrible car crash that nearly ended his career.*

he sternly objected to people clicking cameras while he was playing. My father realized this, and began asking him to pose for photographs during or prior to practice rounds. Ben Hogan always accommodated my father, and you will see some of these posed shots in the accompanying photographs.

After Hogan's automobile accident in 1949, my father made a group photo of all the Masters contestants, which they signed and sent to Ben in the hospital. When he was able to play again, Hogan returned and won the Masters twice. A year or so later, as most golf fans will remember, Hollywood made a movie of his life, *Follow The Sun*, with Glenn Ford starring as Ben Hogan. The producers asked my father for the use of his photographs to help them reproduce authentic scenes and atmosphere. When we saw the film, my father and I were delighted to see how accurately they had recreated his photographs in some of the scenes.

Not many people know that Ben Hogan was responsible for starting the Champions' Dinner. In 1952, as defending champion, Hogan gave a dinner for the past winners and suggested they form a club limited to Masters champions. The idea won immediate favor with Cliff Roberts and Bob Jones, and the Champions' Dinner became a fixture. It is held on Tuesday evenings and is hosted by the previous year's winner, who chooses the menu. This is an occasion when past winners can gather on an evening away from the press and public, a time for swapping stories, and camaraderie. No one is allowed in the room except past champions, the chairman of the club, all of whom wear their green jackets, and yours truly, the photographer.

Oddly, Ben Hogan rarely attended these dinners after he stopped competing, even though many of his contemporaries continued to attend the Masters as honored guests. His great rival, Sam Snead, rarely missed these occasions. Snead is a marvellous storyteller, and has captivated the group for years. Each year, he would perform his famous party trick — kicking the top of the door frame with ease — to demonstrate he was still fit.

In more recent years, the foreign contingent came to dominate the tournament, and this brought interesting consequences to the Champions' Dinner. The year following his dramatic triumph in 1988, Scotsman Sandy Lyle chose to serve haggis, a particularly vile Scottish concoction. I have had the opportunity to taste haggis in Scotland, so I will not describe it other than to say that it is best attempted only after swallowing a strong dose of single-malt

*The first gathering of the Champions' Club took place in 1952, an idea suggested by Ben Hogan who was the defending champion and the first host. The select group included, L-R, back row: Sam Snead, Henry Picard, Jimmy Demaret, Gene Sarazen, Ben Hogan, Horton Smith, Claude Harmon; front row: Byron Nelson, Cliff Roberts, Bob Jones, Craig Wood.*

*Sandy Lyle, in kilt, brandishes a ritual dirk before stabbing the haggis, a dish only a Scot could love, and one that Lyle served as host of the Champions' Dinner in 1989. Dinner companions, Byron Nelson, left, and Ben Crenshaw, right, give him a wide berth.*

whiskey. Dressed in his kilt, Sandy presented the horrid mess, and, removing a dagger from its sheath, performed the ceremonial stabbing of the bladder. I do not believe that anyone outside of Lyle himself, sampled the delicacy. Steak was the preferred substitute of the evening, as I recall.

In spite of the uncertainties of foreign cuisine, I think the Champions' Dinners have been very popular down through the years. The past champions enjoy the opportunity to gather and tell stories, and to make suggestions to the club for improvements in the tournament or in the setup of the golf course. Most of them are good friends, and it is quite obvious that the friendships span generations. These dinners provide the younger winners like Jose Maria Olazabal and Fred Couples an opportunity to socialize with Masters pioneers like Henry Picard and Gene Sarazen, although I have noticed over the years that the young ones tend to sit quietly and listen to the older fellows. Year in and year out, these are very light-hearted gatherings.

Augusta National's caddies are among the best in the world, and they are particularly valuable to Masters contestants because they know the greens so well. The greens, as anyone who has played them knows, are among the trickiest in golf. An experienced caddie might be worth two or three shots a round, and the best ones usually are snapped up by the top players. In his rookie appearance in the Masters, Cary Middlecoff was not so lucky. Middlecoff would go on to win the Masters in 1955, but in 1948 he was just another hot prospect who had won a bunch of tournaments in the South. The Augusta National had run out of caddies and had to assign him a young lad who had been recruited from a neighboring golf course. They dressed him in a caddie uniform and sent him out to shag balls for Cary Middlecoff.

The youngster did fine, but when they got to the first tee, Middlecoff reached out for a club, and the caddie handed him a seven-iron. Cary looked at it, hesitated, then slowly said: "Son, you've never caddied before, have you?" The caddie looked nervous: "Nawssir, I hasn't." "Well, I've never played this tournament before," said Middlecoff, "but we're going to work together just fine." The caddie beamed: "Yassir." Cary replaced the seven-iron in his bag, and said: "Let's begin all over. My name is Dr. Cary Middlecoff. What's yours?" The little caddie exclaimed: "Poe!" Cary was not sure he had heard correctly, and asked: "You mean, like Edgar Allen Poe?" The caddie's eyes grew bright: "I *is* Edgar Allen Poe."

*Cary Middlecoff, the longest straight driver of his day, cracks another one down the fairway in 1955, the year he won a green jacket with relative ease over Ben Hogan and Sam Snead.*

There is a long-running joke at the Augusta National that when people hear a huge roar down in the valley around, say, the thirteenth or the sixteenth, someone will ask, "Wonder what's going on down there?" Someone else will answer, "Aw, Arnold just hitched up his pants." When a roar makes the ground shake, you can be sure that someone made a double eagle, or Arnie just holed a three-footer for par. Sometimes I think Arnold Palmer could make a double bogey and the crowd would cheer.

Has anyone else in the history of the Masters ever stirred that kind of emotion? Not even close. Has anyone ever rivaled Arnold's popularity at the Masters? I don't think so. There is a warm spot in everyone's heart for hometown boy Larry Mize, and we loved it when he won, and Jack Nicklaus earned everyone's respect, and then love, and he is a big favorite, too. But, no, nobody can rival Arnold Palmer. Arnie's Army started at the Augusta National, and believe me, they will still be cheering for Arnold when he is ninety-two and putting with a rake.

One day, I watched as Arnold came to the thirteenth with his army in full throat. He hit what was really an indifferent drive, and when he got to his ball, he stared at the green, tugged on his pants, puffed on his cigarette,

Arnold Palmer reacts to a near miss in the style that endeared him to millions.

and paced back and forth. "Go for it, Arnie," his gallery shouted. He went to his bag and pulled out an iron. Arnold was a long way from the hole, and the "Army" groaned loudly, figuring that their hero was about to lay up on this beautiful but treacherous par-five. Well, Arnie smashed the ball as hard as I have ever seen, and it rode over the creek onto the green and finished within eagle distance. Arnold looked back at the gallery as if to say, "ye of little faith," and they went crazy. I have never seen anything like it. Far from letting them down, once again Arnold had gone for it all and had pulled another one out of the hat, and they loved him for it.

There was one other occasion when the Masters saw that kind of emotion, one incident when someone rivaled Arnold's popularity. It happened in the third round of the 1967 Masters when Ben Hogan shot the back nine in thirty strokes to finish off a brilliant 66. Hogan was by that time a shadow of himself, still the game's great shotmaker but a pitiful figure on the greens. His aching limbs suffering, his pace faltering, he trudged across the hills of Augusta behind one magnificent stroke after another, willing the putts to fall. By the time he made his way slowly up the last hill to the final green, the gallery had grown to thousands, and scarcely one without a lump

# A FAMOUS ROUND

BEN HOGAN'S EMOTIONAL 66 in the third round of the 1967 Masters, drew him into a tie for fourth with Gay Brewer, two strokes behind the leaders:

| | |
|---|---|
| Julius Boros | -5 |
| Bert Yancey | -5 |
| Bobby Nichols | -5 |
| Ben Hogan | -3 |
| Gay Brewer | -3 |
| George Archer | -2 |

Brewer closed with a 67, and won with a score of 280. Hogan finished at 290, tied with Sam Snead and three others, after a final round 77.

*Ben Hogan, age fifty-five, turned back the clock in 1967, scorching the back nine in 30 strokes on Saturday to finish with 66, the low round of the tournament.*

in the throat. Hogan was fifty-five, and everyone present must have sensed they were witnessing his final, glorious gasp. This great man had come back so many times — from failure, from his deadly hook, from death's door itself — and now he was doing it once again. Augustans understood. The cheers kept coming, the sound so deep and resonant it made the hair stand up on your neck.

Jack Nicklaus' astonishing victory in 1986, overtaking the field with that closing 30 on the back nine, was emotional, too, but it was a different kind of emotion. Here was Jack, twenty-four years after his first Masters victory, seeking his sixth green jacket, at the age of forty-six, with his son, Jack Jr., on his bag. It was something. As Jack accepted the trophy, I noticed his mother and sister watching from the sidelines, admiring their golden boy. I realized this would make a good photograph, so I called them over. As they kissed him, one on each cheek, I snapped the picture.

Jack overcame a great deal in his march to glory, more than people may remember. Everyone thinks he had it easy because of his talent, and his comfortable background. I saw something else. When Nicklaus first arrived, people thought, "How dare he beat Arnold Palmer!" There was more than a little animosity toward him. But, Jack won people over with his performances, and his personality warmed along the way. Nicklaus was always on the business end of a golf club, and his rivals knew it. Everybody knew it, and I think that, long ago, the full weight of his accomplishments earned Jack Nicklaus the respect of everyone in golf.

To make a great photograph during competition, a photographer needs both action and reaction. That means he must know something about golf so as to judge when and where a golfer will play the shot, and whether or not it is an important shot in the tournament. To show reaction, some part of the crowd should be in the frame, and it is even better when you can show the player and the crowd in the same shot. It is fairly easy to show this in putting because all the action is contained in the relatively small arena of the green. You learn to wait until the putt is missed or made so you can shoot the reaction. I cannot help but think of Ben Crenshaw's brave holing of that last putt at the last hole in 1995, then falling to his knees and weeping.

Crenshaw's triumph in 1984 was emotional, too, because of his romantic interest in the game and its traditions, and his attachment to the Augusta National, but his second win in 1995 was more poignant still. All week, following the death of his teacher, Harvey Penick, Ben had remained calm and determined. You could see it in his eyes, and in his demeanor. I do not remember ever seeing him so focused. He looked to me as if he were stalking the course, which, up to then, would have been very uncharacteristic of Ben.

I cannot quite put my finger on it, but it was something in his face; he had the look of a champion. The gallery could see it, and on that final day they were all pulling for him. When he took the lead, the fans were part of it, part of him, and when he holed that final putt at eighteen and sank to his knees, his head clasped in his hands, you could almost hear the gallery's collective sigh as their roars began to mount. His posture and their cheers told the whole emotional story.

*Ben Crenshaw, overcome by emotion, is congratulated by his caddie, Carl Jackson, after holing the putt that brought him his second Masters crown in 1995 the same week his lifelong friend and mentor, Harvey Penick, passed away.*

Sometimes, the emotion is so great a photographer may forget to shoot the picture. This has happened to me. I remember Greg Norman arriving at the tee, and having to wait for the group ahead. He leaned his driver against the bench, and began stretching exercises. Standing with his legs stiff and both feet flat on the ground, he bent over until his head touched his legs. He was bent double. I was mesmerized; it did not seem possible he was that supple. I just stood there, my jaw hanging open and my camera by my side, and never made the photograph.

On the other hand, sometimes you can get more than one opportunity to get the same photograph. Let me explain. In 1978, Hubert Green was on the eighteenth green needing to hole a three-footer to tie Gary Player and force a playoff. In those days, few players were better than Hubert from six feet in, but he missed. Later that evening, after the awards ceremony was over, I saw Hubert walking toward the eighteenth green with his putter and a handful of balls. I followed him, and, sure enough, he went back to that same spot on the putting surface, dropped a ball three feet from the cup, and tried to hole it. In the gathering dusk, I shot frame after frame of Hubert's attempts to make

*Hubert Green missed this short one at the last to lose by a stroke in 1978 (right), then came out an hour or two later and tried the same putt five times, and missed them all (above).*

that putt. Of course, he never did. It was not makeable, at least not that day, and not by him.

Cliff Roberts' single-minded obsession with the Masters was something we all took for granted. The protective cloak he spread over the club and the tournament seemed quite normal, if you knew the man, although he did sometimes appear to step over the line. I can vividly recall an example that occurred during the 1970s. This particular year, as happened occasionally, the final round of the Masters fell on Easter Sunday. Frank Chirkinian, the fine producer of the CBS telecast, suggested the tee times be changed to give viewers time to attend church and still see the entire final round on television. Mr. Roberts worked "very closely" with CBS and attended many of the production meetings himself, as he did on this occasion.

When the question arose about the tee times, he grew restless. Obviously, the date for Easter changes each year, a fact that was duly noted by the production executives present. Mr. Roberts wanted to know why. "Find out who's in charge of Easter, and let's see if we can't get them to change the dates," he declared. The people in the meeting were dumbfounded, but the solution was perfectly logical to Cliff Roberts. He saw no reason on either heaven or earth why they could not arrange to have Easter fall on the same

*Frank Chirkinian, for forty years the best producer of golf on television and the man most responsible for bringing the Augusta National and the look of the Masters into America's living rooms.*

date each year, and, more importantly, one that would not conflict with the tournament. As far as Cliff Roberts was concerned, the Masters was bigger than Easter.

In Clifford Roberts' book, there is a reference to an incident that happened in 1969 when Bob Jones was too ill to appear on television for the presentation. Until that time, Jones had always officiated at the television ceremony, which is held in the Butler cabin. Jones had posed questions to the winner and the leading amateur, and was seen to be the tournament host. After Clifford Roberts' death in September of 1977, a CBS official told one of the golf magazines that Mr. Roberts made the decision to bounce Bob Jones from the 1969 telecast, implying that the two men were not such good friends.

"There was no love lost between them," the CBS man was quoted as saying, rather archly. According to this fellow, Mr. Roberts told CBS: "Bob Jones will not make the presentation this year. I will make it, and that's the way it is going to be." CBS was astounded, the story went on, and was left with the delicate and distasteful chore of informing Jones. The magazine's readers were left with the impression that Mr. Roberts wanted to gain national attention for himself.

Here is what actually happened. During that period, Jones was suffering the late stages of his degenerative disease. His facial muscles and hands were horribly crippled. He could barely lift his cigarette holder to his mouth, and was unable to control his saliva. I think Clifford Roberts could not bear to see Jones presented this way to millions of television viewers, and wanted to spare him and the viewers this indignity. It was just too much for Mr. Roberts to bear, and I believe with all my heart that it was out of love and compassion that he acted. Two and a half years later, Bob Jones was dead. There was no question in the minds of those who knew the two men that Clifford Roberts loved Bob Jones, and that Bob Jones had a wonderful, healthy respect for Cliff Roberts' ability to run the club, which he did all by himself those last years.

My photographic work has taken me all over the world, but I have yet to see a tournament that can rival the Masters for sheer beauty, drama, and organization. There is something else about this place. Growing up in Augusta, as we did, allowed us to watch the Masters change and grow over the years from "our" little event in Augusta into a truly international event. To some of us, it is still our event in Augusta, run by Augustans. I think Bob Jones would have approved of this.

The Masters Tournament is such a huge undertaking that people often are surprised at how smoothly it runs. Part of the reason is that the Masters is the only one of the majors held at the same place year after year. Most of the people who work on the committees — housing, food, security, parking, press, television, grounds, etc. — have been doing so for thirty or forty years, some even longer. They know their roles so well they give the impression they could perform them in their sleep. There is never a sense of being rushed or hurried. It is like dancing: When you start out, you are kind of clumsy and your legs grow tired, but after you have been at it for a while, you feel as though you could dance all night. The Augusta National people have been working all these years on the Masters, so it is not surprising that they do it with the greatest of ease. They have been dancing a long time, and they are great dancers.

The Masters Tournament has never been a spectacle. Neither Bob Jones nor Clifford Roberts allowed a carnival atmosphere to develop, and that will not change in the foreseeable future. Its traditions are so strong that people are glad to go along with them. They are a little awed by it all, sometimes, but you can sense that they are pleased. Each generation of spectators seems willing to embrace these traditions. Patrons are quiet and respectful of the golfers at all times, which is not always seen at other tournaments. That is a tradition worth preserving.

To document the history of the Masters has meant a great deal to all the members of my family who have participated over these many years. In this scrapbook, we share some of the good times from these past Masters, along with some of our favorite photographs. When I realize how many thousands of people feel such genuine affection for this place and for the Masters Tournament, I feel very lucky and very humble to have been a part of it, and hope these images bring back fond memories, and a smile or two.

*Morning breaks across the golf course as preparations for another Masters get underway*

First
ANNUAL
INVITATION
TOURNAMENT
AUGUSTA
NATIONAL
GOLF
CLUB
MARCH - 22 - 23 - 24 - 25
AUGUSTA GEORGIA

# PROGRAM NO PROGRAM

MOST TOURNAMENTS, including the majors, publish a fat tournament program in order to generate income, which comes largely from advertising, but there is no souvenir program at the Masters. The club published a Masters program the first two years, a copy of which is shown at left. However, Clifford Roberts decided, with Bob Jones' assent, that the club did not want such commercial ventures associated with the Masters, so it was discontinued. Instead, daily pairing sheets are provided at the tournament for the convenience of patrons. The club does publish a small informational booklet that summarizes past tournaments and records, along with a few words from Bob Jones, and that is the end of it.

*Horton Smith, whose nickname was the Joplin Ghost, won the first Masters in 1934, although it was not called the Masters until 1938. Smith was the first man to win twice, adding the 1936 tournament to his list of credits. A native of Joplin, Missouri, Horton Smith was reckoned one of the finest putters in golf, a skill that is particularly useful at the Augusta National with its large, slick putting surfaces.*

*One of the reasons the Masters is held in early spring is that, when the tournament started in 1934, Augusta was a convenient stopover for sportswriters returning from covering baseball's spring training camps in Florida. Warm relations with the press were encouraged by the tournament's founders, and were reciprocated by the writers, a tradition that continues. As it has for many years, the Golf Writers' Association of America holds its annual meetings at the Masters. This gathering of the golfwriters was photographed outside the tournament office in 1971, and includes, L-R, front row (seated): Fred Corcoran, John Carmichael, Dave Eisenberg, Ben Danforth, Art Spander, Bill Shirley, Jim Trinkle, Maury White, Maury Fitzgerald, Fred Burns, Bill Beck, John Bibb, Nelson Cullenward, Kaye Kessler. Second row (standing): Dick Taylor, Gordon Campbell, Ben Garlikov, Howie Gill, Phil Gundelfinger, Jr., Herb Graffis, Fred Byrod, John Ballentine, Dudley 'Waxo' Green, Bill Inglish, Lincoln Werden, Red Hoffman, Wally Wallis, Bob Green. Third row: Al Ludwick, Jerry Sanders, Dick Slay, Phil Taylor, Joe Greenday, Joe Looney, Herbert Warren Wind, Ralph Moore, Dana Mozley, Tom Place, John Walter, Gerry Finn. Fourth row: Barry McDermott, Doc Giffin, Paul Menneg, Marshall Dann, Roger Barry, Bob Phillips, Cal Brown, Joe Concannon, Bill Davis, Ted Ostermann, Nick Seitz, Ken Bowden.*

TOP

*A sea of automobiles stretches across the fields beside the Augusta National golf course in the early 1950s, by which time the Masters had become a fixture in the hierarchy of golf and one of the most popular destinations for golf fans.*

RIGHT

*Very early, the Club elected to hire Pinkerton's as marshals and security guards rather than use volunteers. Due to their efforts, combined with local police who work to manage the vast numbers of fans and automobiles that flood Augusta during April, the tournaments run very smoothly and efficiently.*

# PRESS COVERAGE

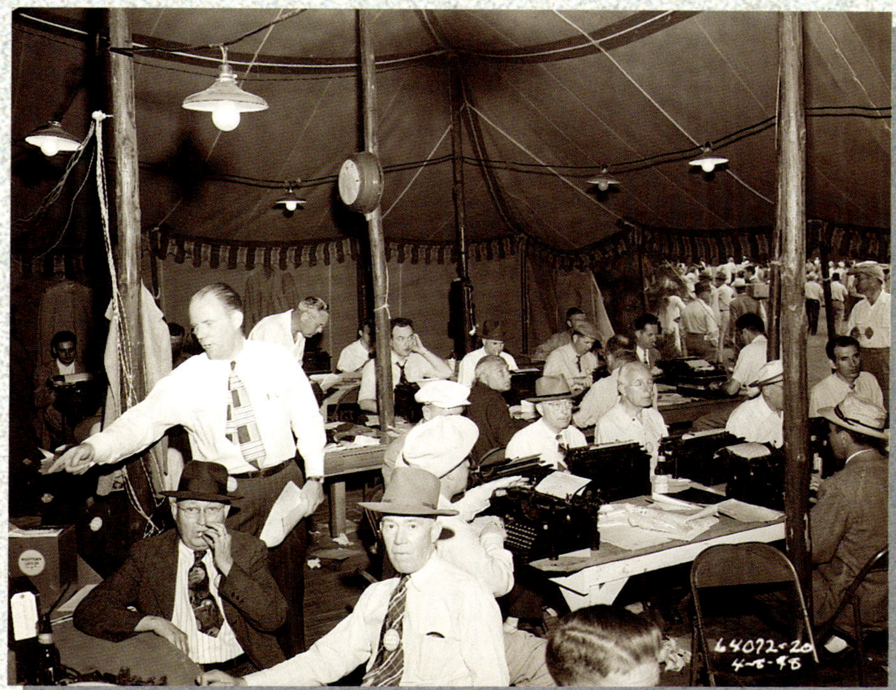


*The old press tent and teletype machines of the 1930s and 1940s gave way to a more or less permanent quonset hut structure of the 1950s and 1960s, below. Today, the press enjoys more spacious quarters in a modern, air-conditioned building built especially for its use.*

*Former U.S. Open winners present for the 1935 Masters gathered for this photograph by Montell; they included, L-R, standing, Willie Macfarlane, Walter Hagen, Bob Jones, Olin Dutra, Billy Burke, and, seated, Gene Sarazen, Tommy Armour, Fred McLeod, George Sargent.*

*Lloyd Mangrum, a perennial favorite to win at Augusta because of his cool demeanor and brilliant putting, came close, but never did. A chain smoker, Mangrum was once scolded by a woman spectator: "Athletes shouldn't smoke," she hissed. Mangrum's reply came from the side of his mouth, a cigarette clamped firmly in his lips: "I'm no ath-ah-leete, lady; I'm a golfer."*

# SCOREBOARDS

*These photos of the scoreboards through the decades show changes in scoring procedures developed first at the Masters. The earliest scoreboard shown here is the one from 1947, top left, still posting the contestant numbers, and scores by hole. By 1950, bottom left, the leader board has dropped contestant numbers, and adopted a scoring system closer to the modern one. By 1960, top right, the Masters had adopted a system of posting figures representing the number of strokes over or under par a player was at that moment. Red figures indicate number of strokes under par, green figures the number of strokes over par, or scores at even par, as in the modern board, bottom right.*

*This system, started at the Masters, has been adopted universally by modern professional tournament golf.*

MASTERS LEADING SCORES
HOLES
PAR
PREV. SCORE
ROSBURG
PALMER.A
SNEAD
LEONARD
PLAYER
CASPER
VENTURI
BEMAN
HOGAN
NICKLAUS
LEGEND
RED FIGURES - UNDER PAR
GREEN ZERO - EVEN PAR
GREEN FIGURES - OVER PAR
SCORES AS SHOWN ON A CUMULATIVE BASIS
NOTES
FINSTERWALD 69
CLAUDE HARMON 69
SOUCHAK 34 OUT
HAWKINS 69

LEADERS
HOLE
PAR
PRIOR
LYLE
CRENSHAW
CALCAVECCHIA
LANGER
COUPLES
ZOELLER
POOLEY
STADLER
NORMAN
BALLESTEROS
THRU 14
BALLESTEROS 0
STADLER 5

TOP

*The Texas connection, L-R, Jimmy Demaret, Byron Nelson, and Ben Hogan, seated on bench with host Bob Jones, accounted for seven Masters titles among them, and these four men were, with Sam Snead, the principal reasons for the emergence of the Masters as the fourth "major" championship of professional golf.*

RIGHT

*Claude Harmon, head pro at the Winged Foot Golf Club in Mamaroneck, New York, was a native of Savannah, Georgia, and something of a favorite son in 1948 when he slipped in with a five stroke victory over Cary Middlecoff and slipped into his own green coat, the first club pro, and the first homebred, to win the Masters. Here he plays from the edge of Rae's Creek, at the twelfth hole, where he salvaged a bogey; he visited the creek again at the next hole, but managed a par.*

*Contestants arriving by train, a frequent occurance in the 1930s and 1940s, were met in style by chauffered auto.*

*Effectively retired from the game for a decade, Bob Jones could relax at the Masters and watch the new talent in golf; here he sits on the knoll above the putting green watching players putt and chip.*

LEFT

*The matchless rhythm and grace of this golf swing could belong to only one man, the incomparable Sam Snead, here launching an iron approach from the left side of the fairway while watched intently by the gallery.*

BOTTOM

*British star Henry Cotton runs through the scorecard with Bob Jones during Cotton's first visit to the Masters in 1948, the year he won his third British Open.*

*The 1948 field assembled informally on the practice putting green for this memento, my first photograph at the Masters. The players are, L-R, seated in front row: Dick Chapman, Art Bell, Jimmy Demaret, Byron Nelson, Ralph Guldahl, Herman Keiser, Horton Smith, Gene Sarazen, Craig Wood, Henry Picard; seated, second row: Bobby Locke, Lawson Little, Al Smith, Lloyd Mangrum, Chick Harbert, Lew Worsham, Harry Todd, Skip Alexander, Johnny Palmer, Felice Torza, Toney Penna, Freddie Haas (hidden behind Penna), Skee Riegel, Harvie Ward, Bud Ward. Standing: Henry Cotton, Johnny Bulla, Sam Byrd, Ed Furgol, Claude Harmon, Cary Middlecoff, Herman Barron, Bob Hamilton, Jimmy McHale, Jug McSpaden, Vic Ghezzi, Johnny Farrell, Dutch Harrison (partially visible behind Farrell), Bobby Jones, Jack Selby, Ellsworth Vines, Denny Shute, Duke Gibson, Chandler Harper, Bill Nary, Dick Metz, Ben Hogan, Jim Ferrier, Joe Kirkwood, Sam Snead, Ed Dudley. This was Bobby Jones' last appearance as a competitor.*

*Charlie Coe, the raw-boned wonder from Oklahoma, had the best record among amateurs who played in the Masters. He nearly won in 1961, finishing a stroke behind the winner, Gary Player, and three times finished in the top ten; six times he was the low amateur in a span that covered twenty-two years from 1949 to 1970, a tournament amateur record likely to stand.*

*Billy Joe Patton, left, two years after his near-victory in the Masters, lends encouragement to fellow amateur Ken Venturi in 1956 after Venturi stormed into the lead after two rounds, a lead he kept well into the fourth round before stumbling to an 80 and losing by one.*

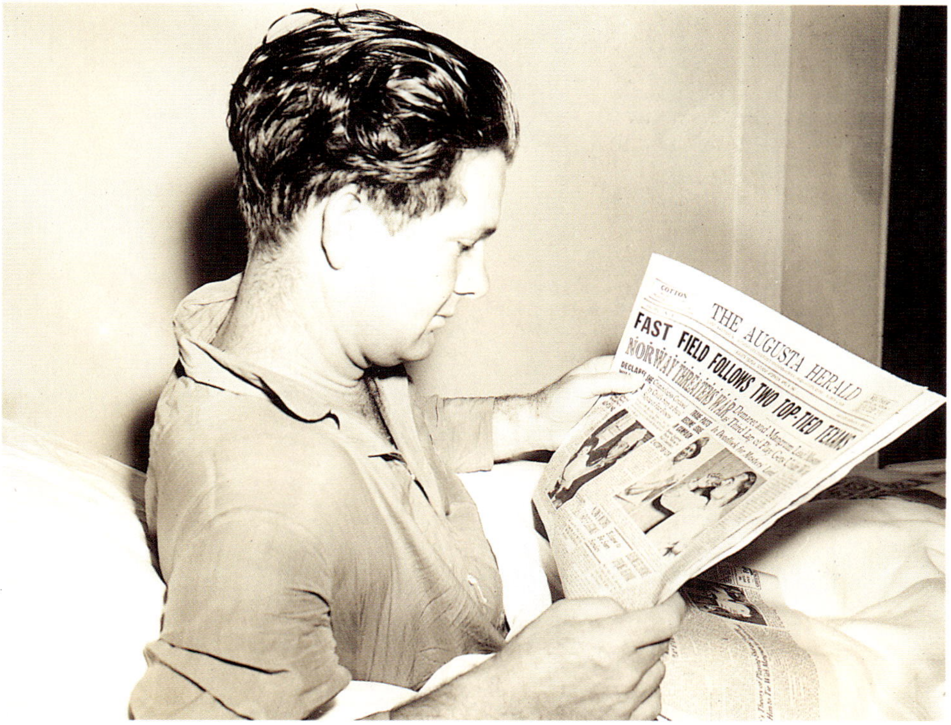


*Hospitalized briefly after the second round, Jimmy Demaret learns from the headlines in the newspaper that he and fellow Texan Lloyd Mangrum lead the Masters at the half-way point in 1940. Jimmy climbed out of bed to win his first of three Masters.*

*Whenever Tommy Armour practiced, other pros stopped to watch his action, much as a later generation did with Ben Hogan. Here, his admirers include Grantland Rice, resting on shooting stick, Jug McSpaden, dark sweater, Henry Picard, with legs crossed, and Jimmy Thomson, white sweater, as Armour warms up at the 1936 Masters.*

# AUGUSTA PROMOTES THE MASTERS

*In the early days of the Masters, the merchants and citizens of Augusta got behind the tournament in a big way, with parades, floats, a fancy social called the Golf Ball, and townwide promotions to sell tickets that included the election of "Miss Golf." In the accompanying photos, Bob Jones waves from the lead car during a parade, followed by floats with Miss Augusta and her court, Miss Coca Cola and hers, a billboard sponsored by the Merchants Association promotes the tournament, car stickers announce "Just Saw the Masters Tournament," and a giant scorecard is erected on Broad Street downtown to record daily scores and progress of the tournament for shoppers and townspeople.*

*The Silver Scot, The Haig, and the Emperor Jones dominated American golf between World War I and the Depression; between them, Tommy Armour, Walter Hagen, and Bobby Jones won seven U.S. Opens, six PGA Championships, and eight British Opens over this stretch of a dozen years, all of which earned them these spots in the lockerrooom of the Augusta National Golf Club in 1936.*

# HIS MASTERS SCORES

WHEN HE RETIRED FROM competitive golf in 1930, Bobby Jones was the game's acknowledged master. Although he never again competed in serious competition, he did play in another dozen "majors" because of his role as the host and main attraction of the early Masters Tournaments. Jones' participation in the Masters was vital to its growing acceptance by press and public. In the first tournament in 1934, Jones finished with a pair of 72s, which allowed him to tie for thirteenth with two old, familiar rivals, Walter Hagen and Denny Shute. In his twelve Masters appearances, Bob Jones was unable to improve on this score, although he managed to duplicate his single-round best of 72 in 1935, 1938, 1942, and 1946.

***Bobby Jones' scores, by year:***

| YEAR | SCORES | PLACE |
|---|---|---|
| 1934 | 76-74-72-72—294 | T13 |
| 1935 | 74-72-73-78—297 | T25 |
| 1936 | 78-78-73-77—306 | T33 |
| 1937 | 79-74-73-77—303 | T29 |
| 1938 | 76-74-72-75—297 | T16 |
| 1939 | 76-77-78-73—304 | T33 |
| 1940 | 79-76—WD | |
| 1941 | 76-74-78-79—307 | T39 |
| 1942 | 72-75-79-78—304 | T28 |
| 1946 | 75-72-77-78—302 | T32 |
| 1947 | 75-79-78-80—312 | T55 |
| 1948 | 76-81-79-79—315 | T49 |

*Bob Jones, here getting an earful from The Squire, Gene Sarazen, played in a dozen Masters, the last in 1948.*

# BING CROSBY'S HOUSE

WHEN BING CROSBY visited the Masters for the first time, he decided to rent a house rather than stay in a hotel. Golfing buddies Toney Penna and Jimmy Demaret had been after Crosby for some time to visit the Masters and, finally, in the mid-1950s, he agreed to come. He brought his pal, Phil Harris, with him. Penna and Demaret were on the staff of the Macgregor Golf Company, then headed by Clarence Rickey, who was a cousin of the Brooklyn Dodgers' general manager, Branch Rickey. Clarence's son, Bob Rickey, was Macgregor's advertising and promotion man, and helped Penna find a suitable house for Crosby. In addition to Penna and Demaret, Macgregor's stable of stars included Ben Hogan, Byron Nelson, Jay and Lionel Hebert, Jack Burke, and Mike Souchak, and later would include Jack Nicklaus. Most of them were Crosby's pals as well, and they would all wind up at Bing's house after play had finished. Watching the banter at these informal parties during the week, Bob Rickey had a brainstorm. The following year, he rented the Goodrich house in the hill section of Augusta, which gave the Macgregor staff a comfortable, roomy place to entertain its clients and friends. Bob invited me to the first party to take pictures, and I was impressed because all the Macgregor stars were in attendance. The Macgregor house was the place to be that week, and was crowded almost every night. Toney Penna cooked spaghetti for anyone who was hungry, and the drinks flowed. It was the beginning of a trend, soon to be copied by every major manufacturer, supplier, publisher, and association in golf. Today, the Masters Housing Agency handles requests from twenty thousand individuals and corporations for private accommodations, and acts as broker for more than six thousand home owners who rent their property at very lucrative rates during Masters Week. This activity contributes about $10 million per annum to Augusta's economy, all thanks to Bing Crosby's house and Bob Rickey's initiative.

*Bing Crosby, a low handicap golfer who once competed in the British Amateur Championship, is greeted by Masters chairman Clifford Roberts before heading out to the course.*

A crowd gathers underneath the spreading oak at Masters time to relax, socialize, and reminisce about the game.

Ben Hogan holes his final putt at eighteen for 68 and victory in 1951, watched by his playing partner Byron Nelson, at right. The periscopes visible in the foreground were an experiment, and were banned when Cliff Roberts decided they were "unsightly."

*In the locker room, Lloyd Mangrum, top, explains to Herman Keiser, and Jack Burke, bottom, to anyone who'll listen how they "knocked it this close."*

# RINGER SCORES

SO OBSESSED WITH PERFECTION was Ben Hogan that he once dreamed of holing seventeen tee shots, just missing a perfect round when his 440-yard drive on the eighteenth lipped out. Leave it to Hogan to claim an all-time ringer score. A ringer score is a career best on a given hole, so named because when it occurs it is usually circled on the scorecard. This can be kept both for an individual player, and for a golf course. Those who keep track of such things at the Augusta National have compiled the ringer scores from the Masters, which are listed below. Through 1996, eagles have been scored on all the holes, double-eagles three times. Fourteen holes-in-one have been recorded, but only one at the long, tough fourth hole. Only once, also, has the par-four eleventh, with its fateful greenside pond, been holed in two. The author of that majestic stroke was the short-hitting Jerry Barber, something of a magician with long irons and fairway woods, who accomplished the feat in 1962.

| HOLE | PLAYER | YEAR | SCORE | MATCHED BY |
|---|---|---|---|---|
| 1 | Frank Moore | 1940 | 2 | Roberto deVicenzo 1968, and two others. |
| 2 | Olin Dutra | 1935 | 3 | Many others (over two dozen). |
| 3 | Bruce Crampton | 1974 | 2 | Curtis Strange 1985, Ray Floyd 1991, and three others. |
| 4 | Jeff Sluman | 1992 | 1 | Only eagle. |
| 5 | Art Wall | 1974 | 2 | Three others and TWICE by Jack Nicklaus in 1995. |
| 6 | Billy Joe Patton | 1954 | 1 | Duke Gibson 1954, Charles Coody 1972. |
| 7 | Dick Mayer | 1955 | 2 | Jack Nicklaus 1976, and two others. |
| 8 | Bruce Devlin | 1967 | 2 | Only double eagle. |
| 9 | Earl Stewart | 1954 | 2 | Curtis Strange 1980, Steve Jones 1991. |
| 10 | Dick Metz | 1940 | 2 | Doug Ford 1960, and two others. |
| 11 | Jerry Barber | 1962 | 2 | Only eagle. |
| 12 | Claude Harmon | 1947 | 1 | Bill Hyndman 1959, Curtis Strange 1988. |
| 13 | Jeff Maggert | 1994 | 2 | Only double eagle. |
| 14 | Frank Stranahan | 1954 | 2 | Ray Floyd 1984, Brett Ogle 1993. |
| 15 | Gene Sarazen | 1935 | 2 | Only double eagle. |
| 16 | Ross Somerville | 1934 | 1 | Corey Pavin 1992, Ray Floyd 1996, and four others. |
| 17 | Takaaki Kono | 1969 | 2 | Tommy Nakajima 1989. |
| 18 | Felice Torza | 1948 | 2 | Denis Hutchinson 1962, Jim Colbert 1974 |
| OUT 17 | IN 16 | TOTAL 33 | | |

# HIGH SCORES FOR EACH HOLE

THE CAPACITY OF THE Augusta National golf course to extract a high score from any man on any hole is well known by the competitors in the Masters, and is illustrated by this list of the highest scores recorded for each hole during the Masters. These scores are not necessarily as high as you might expect, although the two holes on which the highest score has been recorded are probably the most treacherous on the course, the twelfth and the thirteenth. To appear on the list is no disgrace, because it tells us less about the prowess of the players than it does the dangers lurking on every hole. These are testaments to the subtle, sometimes exasperating tests of championship golf that Jones and Mackenzie put to the player at nearly every turn. The high scores for each hole:

| HOLE | PLAYER | YEAR | SCORE | MATCHED BY |
|---|---|---|---|---|
| 1 | Frank Stranahan | 1952 | 7 | Dow Finsterwald & Craig Wood 1952, and eight others. |
| 2 | Sam Byrd | 1948 | 10 | |
| 3 | Douglas Clarke | 1980 | 8 | |
| 4 | Dave Eichelberger | 1965 | 7 | Nathaniel Crosby 1982. |
| 5 | Bill Campbell | 1957 | 8 | Sam Parks 1957, Jerry Barber 1964. |
| 6 | Jose M. Olazabal | 1991 | 7 | |
| 7 | DeWitt Weaver | 1972 | 8 | Richard von Tacky 1981. |
| 8 | Frank Walsh | 1935 | 12 | |
| 9 | Jack Selby | 1948 | 8 | Richard Davies 1963. |
| 10 | Craig Wood | 1954 | 8 | Bill Hoffer 1984. |
| 11 | Dow Finsterwald | 1952 | 9 | Bo Wininger 1958, William Moody 1980. |
| 12 | Tom Weiskopf | 1980 | 13 | |
| 13 | Tommy Nakajima | 1978 | 13 | |
| 14 | Nick Price | 1993 | 8 | |
| 15 | Jumbo Ozaki | 1987 | 11 | |
| 16 | Herman Barron | 1950 | 11 | |
| 17 | Ernie Vossler | 1956 | 7 | Lionel Hebert 1961, Doug Ford 1995, and five others. |
| 18 | Denny Shute | 1959 | 8 | Jumbo Ozaki 1994, Ian Baker-Finch 1995. |
| OUT 75 | IN 88 | | TOTAL 163 | |

*Tommy Aaron peers into the brook at thirteen where his ball, like so many others, has come to rest. The temptation is strong to play the ball from such shallow water, but is best resisted, as Curtis Strange and others have found.*

*Doug Ford, master of the wedge, blasts from the bunker beside the eighteenth green, watched by playing partner Cary Middlecoff; the ball, just visible above the cloud of sand, is destined for the cup and a dramatic birdie which capped a closing 66 and brought him the Masters title in 1957.*

*Jimmy Demaret, watched by playing partner Bob Jones, lines up a putt on the ninth green in 1940, the year Demaret won the first of his three Masters titles.*

*Hole cutter and cups stand at the ready, as tournament officials, including the USGA's P. J. Boatwright, below, confer over hole locations.*

# THE GREEN JACKET

EVERYONE WHO HAS SEEN the Masters knows that the winner is presented with a custom-tailored version of the club's green jacket. It was not always so. In the early days of the tournament, winners received a check, pieces of crystal for outstanding performance in various categories, and had their names engraved on the Masters trophy, but it was not until 1949 that a green jacket became part of the spoils. According to Clifford Roberts' book, no one can remember whose idea this was, but we do know that the first recipient was Sam Snead, seated below with his winner's jacket.

The green coats are suppossed to be kept and worn only on club grounds. However, the winner of the Masters is permitted to take his green jacket away with him for one year, after which it cannot be removed from the club. Occassionally, players have been known to breach this rule. Recently, Gary Player revealed that he still has the green coat presented for his first victory in 1961. Gary, who also won the Masters in 1974 and 1978, said he took his green jacket home with him to Johannesburg, South Africa, and it has remained in his closet ever since. "After learning that the coat was in South Africa, Cliff Roberts telephoned me and asked me to bring it back. I told him it was a long way to travel, and suggested that if he wanted it that badly, he should come and get it," said Gary. "He got a chuckle out of that and told me never to wear it in public."

*TOP*

*Gary Player donning the green jacket at the awards ceremony in 1978.*

*LEFT*

*Sam Snead in the first winners jacket in 1949. Frank Christian, Sr., left in the foreground, captures the moment.*

*The Masters Trophy, a replica of the historic clubhouse rendered in solid silver, is mounted on a circular pedestal of silver into which are engraved the winners' names. The trophy is exhibited in the rear foyer of the clubhouse.*

# PLAYOFFS

IN THE SIXTY MASTERS TOURNAMENTS between 1934 and 1996, eleven have gone to playoffs. The one we never saw, but wished we had — the sad scorekeeping error visited upon one of golf's finest gentlemen, Roberto de Vicenzo — would have made it an even dozen. The first Masters playoff occurred, as everyone surely knows, in the tournament's second year in 1935 when, after his famous double eagle in the fourth round, Gene Sarazen defeated Craig Wood in thirty-six holes, 144 to 149. It was the custom in golf then to stage playoffs, especially in the major championships, over thirty-six holes, but this was the only time it was done in the Masters. For the next four decades, Masters playoffs were conducted over eighteen holes. Beginning in 1979, with television the prime reason, playoffs were changed to sudden-death, beginning at the tenth hole and continuing until a winner is decided. Since that time, no playoff has gone past the eleventh hole; indeed, four of the five sudden-death playoffs have ended at the eleventh green.

*Roberto de Vicenzo accepted his misfortune with grace following the scorecard penalty that cost him a chance to tie a fast-closing Bob Goalby and force a playoff for the 1968 Masters title. Seated at left is Goalby, and at far right, low amateur Vinny Giles. Standing at Roberto's left is club steward Bowman Milligan, holding the green jacket that will shortly be placed on the winner.*

*The first Masters playoff, and the only one at thirty-six holes, was between Gene Sarazen and Craig Wood, at right, signing his scorecard after losing, 144 to 149.*

*Hogan drives from the first tee to start the 1942 playoff with Byron Nelson, standing at left.*

By many accounts, the greatest playoff in Masters history was the one in 1942 between Byron Nelson and Ben Hogan. Nelson had threaded a miracle five-iron through the branches of trees and onto the green at the seventy-second hole to make par and force a playoff, the third time the two ex-caddies from the Glen Gardens club in Fort Worth, Texas, would meet in head-to-head competition; Nelson won all three. By 1942, Byron already had won three majors, including a Masters, and Hogan none, although he had been the leading money winner the previous two years and would be again in 1942. Many of the players stayed over on Monday — a rare occurrence — to watch the pair generally regarded as the best in golf go after one another. After five holes, Hogan led by three strokes and played the next eleven holes in one under par. Over that stretch, Nelson picked up five strokes and won the playoff, 69 to 70. Hogan would not win the Masters for another decade. It was Nelson's second, and last, Masters title.

# PLAYOFFS (CONTINUED)

Twelve years later, Ben Hogan was involved in another epic, this time with Sam Snead. By 1954, Hogan had won four U.S. Opens, and Snead none, but Sam had won four other majors to Ben's three and would win this one, too, 70 to 71. If it was not the most dramatic playoff at the Masters, it was certainly a titanic struggle between the two players who then stood at the pinnacle of golf. Fred Russell, the veteran sportswriter of the *Nashville Banner*, was on the sidelines and stated that "it was the best exhibition of precision golf I've witnessed in golf; neither Snead nor Hogan was ever in the rough." Both Snead and Hogan were forty-three; it would be the last major title for either of them.

If there has not been a better playoff than the one in 1942 between Nelson and Hogan, there can scarcely have been a more dramatic one than the shocker in 1987 when Larry Mize first peeled the hide from Seve Ballesteros at ten, and then administered the thunderclap at eleven that left Greg Norman, and just about everyone else in golf, transfixed. It was one of the most competitive Masters in history, with three others, including Ben Crenshaw and a fast-closing Jodie Mudd, finishing at 286, just a stroke behind the playoff trio. Mize was steadier than his opponents at the tenth, where Ballesteros missed a short par putt and wearily trudged back to the clubhouse while the others moved to the eleventh. Mize's approach went wide onto the lawn at the right of the green, while Norman's found the putting surface. Mize faced a dangerous chip of forty-five yards across a glassy surface toward the dark, menacing pond which lay beyond the cup. A firm stroke with a wedge, a couple of low bounces onto the green and a nice long roll, and in she went, and down went Norman. It was as sudden and as final as a gunshot, and Norman's putt missed, as everyone knew it must. It will be a long time before we witness another finish like that one.

Nick Faldo is the only man with two playoff victories to his credit, and he did them back to back, as well, in 1989 and 1990. Both of them ended at the eleventh, and on both occasions Nick holed long putts to win. In the first playoff, he dodged a bullet at the tenth when Scott Hoch missed a two-footer for par that would have given him the title. In that tournament, Crenshaw, Ballesteros, and Norman were crawling down the leaders' necks at the finish, coming within one stroke of the playoff. The following year, Faldo faced the formidable Ray Floyd, himself a Masters winner in 1976 and no stranger to pressure. At the eleventh, both men drove well, with Floyd first to play. His approach, pulled only slightly, arched too closely to the greenside pond that invites just such a shot, and in he went as all who gamble with this sullen hazard will do. That opening was enough, and Faldo's knowledge of the putting surface brought him the rest of the way home.

*Larry Mize chipped to the eleventh green and, after a journey of forty-five yards, the ball fell in for a birdie that shook his opponent, Greg Norman, and everyone who was watching.*

# PLAYOFFS (CONTINUED)

Arnold Palmer, Jack Nicklaus, and Billy Casper each have scored a playoff victory in the Masters, but none has been particularly dramatic. Casper won by the largest margin, five strokes over Gene Littler in 1970, while Palmer in 1962 and Nicklaus in 1966 glided to fairly comfortable wins. In 1962, Arnold dusted Gary Player by three shots and good friend Dow Finsterwald by nine with a sizzling 68, and followed Jimmy Demaret and Sam Snead as three-time Masters winners. Nicklaus in 1966 cruised in with a 70 to beat Tommy Jacobs by two and Gay Brewer by eight in another three-way playoff.

## THE PLAYOFFS FOR THE MASTERS

| YEAR | WINNER | SCORE | RUNNER-UP AND SCORE |
|---|---|---|---|
| 1935 | Gene Sarazen (36 holes) | 144 | Craig Wood 149 |
| 1942 | Byron Nelson (18 holes) | 69 | Ben Hogan 70 |
| 1954 | Sam Snead (18 holes) | 70 | Ben Hogan 71 |
| 1962 | Arnold Palmer (18 holes) | 68 | Gary Player 71, Dow Finsterwald 77 |
| 1966 | Jack Nicklaus (18 holes) | 70 | Tommy Jacobs 72, Gay Brewer 78 |
| 1970 | Billy Casper (18 holes) | 69 | Gene Littler 74 |
| 1979 | Fuzzy Zoeller | 4-3 | Ed Sneed 4-4, Tom Watson 4-4 |
| 1982 | Craig Stadler | 4 | Dan Pohl 5 |
| 1987 | Larry Mize | 4-3 | Greg Norman 4-4, Seve Ballesteros 5 |
| 1989 | Nick Faldo | 5-3 | Scott Hoch 5-4 |
| 1990 | Nick Faldo | 4-4 | Ray Floyd 4-5 |

*Ben Hogan drives from the tee during the playoff with Sam Snead, watching at left, in 1954; the pair played flawlessly, Snead winning by a single stroke.*

*Fuzzy Zoeller leaps in triumph after holing a birdie putt at the eleventh green to win a playoff with Ed Sneed and Tom Watson, the first one at sudden-death, then checks his winner's jacket for the owner's name.*

*Earlybird spectators stake out choice seats behind the sixteenth green, even before the dewsweepers arrive.*

*The ill-fated Greg Norman misses this putt at the last which would have tied him with Jack Nicklaus in 1986.*

*Extra tall nets, installed at the end of the practice range to contain the mammoth drives of John Daly (shown above driving to the fourth green), only provoked him, and others, who boomed shots over the nets and onto Washington Road.*

# PAR-3 WINNERS

THE PAR-3 TOURNAMENT began in 1960, and the inaugural event was won, to no one's surprise, by Sam Snead. The graceful Snead was forty-seven, and would win it again in 1974 at the age of sixty-one. The Ageless One nearly won again in 1991, a month shy of his seventy-ninth birthday, but lost in a playoff to Rocco Mediate. Isao Aoki and Jay Haas are the others to have won twice, Haas at age twenty-one as an amateur in 1976 and again in 1996 as a seasoned pro.

Other interesting highlights: Raymond Floyd played in twenty-five Masters before winning the Par-3 contest in 1990, his twenty-sixth appearance. The record for the nine-hole tournament is 20, seven-under par, set in 1965 by Art Wall and matched by Gay Brewer in 1973. Claude Harmon scored consecutive aces in 1968, and, through 1996, Gary Player had recorded a total of three holes-in-one, the most by any player. Beginning in 1961, Byron Nelson scored twenty consecutive threes, a record. Between 1972 and 1980, Billy Casper had nine straight subpar rounds, a record, and from 1961 to 1994 Casper recorded nineteen career subpar rounds. The oldest player to beat par was Snead, who covered the nine-hole course in three-under 24 at age seventy-eight in 1991. The biggest margin of victory was three strokes, by Art Wall in 1965.

In the thirty-seven renewals through 1996, no one has managed to win both the Par-3 Tournament and the Masters in the same year — just another of golf's oddities. Ben Crenshaw came closest in 1987, finishing a stroke behind at the end of four rounds, although he would have had to survive a four-way playoff with Larry Mize, the eventual Masters champion, the eternally star-crossed Greg Norman, and a game but fading Seve Ballesteros.

*Jay Haas receives the crystal trophy from Buzz Davis (left) and Haley Roberts (right) for winning the Par-3 Tournament in 1996, his second; Jay also won this event as an amateur in 1976.*

# The Par-3 Contest winners (1960—1996)

| YEAR | WINNER | YEAR | WINNER | YEAR | WINNER |
|---|---|---|---|---|---|
| 1960 | Sam Snead | 1973 | Gay Brewer | 1985 | Hubert Green |
| 1961 | Deane Beman * | 1974 | Sam Snead | 1986 | Gary Koch |
| 1962 | Bruce Crampton | 1975 | Isao Aoki | 1987 | Ben Crenshaw |
| 1963 | George Bayer | 1976 | Jay Haas * | 1988 | Tommy Nakajima |
| 1964 | Labron Harris, Jr. * | 1977 | Tom Weiskopf | 1989 | Bob Gilder |
| 1965 | Art Wall | 1978 | Lou Graham | 1990 | Raymond Floyd |
| 1966 | Terry Dill | 1979 | Joe Inman | 1991 | Rocco Mediate |
| 1967 | Arnold Palmer | 1980 | Johnny Miller | 1992 | Davis Love III |
| 1968 | Bob Rosburg | 1981 | Isao Aoki | 1993 | Chip Beck |
| 1969 | Bob Lunn | 1982 | Tom Watson | 1994 | Vijay Singh |
| 1970 | Harold Henning | 1983 | Hale Irwin | 1995 | Hal Sutton |
| 1971 | Dave Stockton | 1984 | Tommy Aaron | 1996 | Jay Haas |
| 1972 | Steve Melnyk | | | | |

* Amateurs

*The Champions' Dinner in 1960, hosted by defending champion Art Wall, was attended by the winners of all but one Masters up until then, L-R, seated: Horton Smith, Gene Sarazen, Sam Snead, Jimmy Demaret, Bob Jones, Art Wall, Claude Harmon, Doug Ford, Arnold Palmer, and Clifford Roberts, in back; standing: Jack Burke, Henry Picard, Craig Wood, Cary Middlecoff, Byron Nelson, Herman Keiser, and Ben Hogan. Missing was Ralph Guldahl.*

*By the 1990s, the Champions Club had grown too large to photograph seated at the table, so we devised this arrangement at the end of the room. Present for the 1996 dinner were, L-R, seated: Sam Snead, Byron Nelson, Herman Keiser, Henry Picard, chairman Jack Stephens, Ben Crenshaw, Gene Sarazen, Arnold Palmer, Jack Nicklaus. Second row: Charles Coody, Raymond Floyd, Bernhard Langer, Doug Ford, Seve Ballesteros, Gary Player, Tom Watson, Billy Casper, Nick Faldo. Back row: Larry Mize, Ian Woosnam, Art Wall, Sandy Lyle, Craig Stadler, Bob Goalby, Fred Couples, Gay Brewer, Tommy Aaron, and Fuzzy Zoeller.*

# BEN HOGAN

*Glaring intently at the second tee are Ben Hogan and Arnold Palmer, masters indeed, representing two great eras in professional golf.*

*Ben Hogan is interviewed by CBS Radio's sports correspondent Harry Wismer in 1951, the year Hogan won his first Masters. After three rounds, Sam Snead and Skee Riegel led the field at five under par; Hogan was one stroke back. While Snead skied to an 80, including an eight at the dangerous eleventh, Hogan carved out an error-free round of 68, beating Riegel by two strokes, adding the Masters to his two U. S. Open and two PGA Championships. Hogan would win the U. S. Open again that summer, but his greatest year was to come.*

*In his prime, Hogan weighed barely 140 pounds, yet was one of the game's longest hitters, when he wanted to be; the reasons were his superior flexibility, which allowed him to swing at enormous speed, and his huge hands, which were strong enough to control this speed. Before a round, he was very cooperative in posing for my father and others, with the understanding that they would not bother him on the golf course.*

*Hogan's putting skills declined perceptibly over the years, and he once suggested the pros play to flagsticks cut into the greens, without cups; the closest to the flag would win the hole. In his last decade of competition, Hogan had difficulty drawing the putter back, but always tried to overcome the "yips;" below he gets a putting tip from fellow-Texan Jack Burke Jr., one of the best with the flat stick.*

TOP

*This photograph of Jimmy Demaret and Ben Hogan sipping a soda with two straws was made by my father in 1939 or 1940, and is one of my favorites. They were both famous young golfers, fellow Texans, and handsome enough to be movie stars.*

BOTTOM

*Ben relaxes in the players' locker room during his last appearance in 1967.*

LEFT

*Golf legends Walter Hagen, left, and Francis Ouimet were paired in the first round in 1941, the only year Ouimet played in the Masters. Though both men returned scores in the 80s and withdrew, it was an historic matchup of the man who put professional golf in the first class seats with the man who lit the fire of American amateur golf in 1913 when he beat the best of Great Britain, Harry Vardon and Ted Ray.*

BOTTOM

*A refreshment truck, supplied by the YMCA, served duty as an early snack bar, enjoyed here by, L-R, Tommy Armour, Bob Jones, Edward, the Duke of Windsor, Gene Sarazen, and Walter Hagen. The year was 1935.*

*Samuel Jackson Snead, whose graceful swing and prodigious length earned him the nickname, Slammin' Sammy, was all decked out in the attire of the day, including necktie and felt hat, when he made his first Masters appearance in 1937. Snead nearly won the tournament in 1939, setting a record of 280, which only held up for an hour or so because Ralph Guldahl fired 33 on the back to finish one stroke better, and Sam would wait ten more years before winning it.*

*Byron Nelson was a virtual unknown in 1935, having earned his way into the Masters with a surprise victory over the better-known Lawson Little in a San Francisco tournament earlier that year. Two years later, Byron would win the Masters, and his later exploits would inspire O. B. Keeler to dub him Lord Byron.*

# ARNOLD PALMER

TOP LEFT

*A young Arnold Palmer, brash and muscular, made his first appearance in the Masters in 1955 following his victory in the U.S. Amateur championship a year earlier, and finished tenth. No one knew it then, but a legend was building.*

BOTTOM LEFT

*Still the magnetic figure in his sixties, Arnold's love affair with the Augusta National and the Masters is a mirror of his place in American golf.*

BOTTOM RIGHT

*Palmer proved as adept with the press as he was with an adoring public, and is seen here in an impromptu interview after his second win in 1960.*

TOP

*The exuberance so characteristic of Arnold Palmer's performance was never more evident than on the last green in 1964 when he holed this birdie putt to capture his fourth Masters; behind him, the "Army," born here at the Augusta National, rises as one.*

BOTTOM

*Arnold Palmer, a green jacket, and a Cadillac, posed in front of the clubhouse entrance, all of which have become symbols of the Masters.*

*You could get a pretty good argument over who was the best putter among this trio: Sarazen, at left, the boldest putter in golf before Palmer; Jones, at right, the most dangerous long putter in history; and Hagen, putting, the coolest and most confident finisher before Nicklaus.*

# BILLY JOE PATTON

*Amateur Billy Joe Patton came to the thirteenth hole on the last day in 1954 leading the Masters, with Sam Snead and Ben Hogan at his heels. His drive finished on the hill at the right side of the fairway, posing the classic question at this short par-five: to try for the green or not? Patton, saying he didn't come to the Masters to play safe, went for the green with wood, top left, but his ball bounced into the creek bed in front of the green, above, where Patton and officials, who included the USGA's Joe Dey, searched for it. Patton found his ball, and after rolling up his trousers, chose to pitch from the ditch, at left, but the ball stayed in and Patton wound up with double bogey seven, dropping him from the lead. Another gamble at fifteen led to more water and a bogey, and Patton lost his bid for the Masters by one shot. Though winning as an amateur would have placed him in high company indeed, in losing Patton gained his own piece of immortality.*

*The gallery at the 1949 Masters got a close look at the players, a view they would not get today since gallery ropes are used to contain the spectators.*

*According to Bob Jones, Gene Sarazen was "the kind of player who might go around the course like a tiger, when the mood struck," and Sarazen proved it once again during practice rounds in 1935 when he turned four rounds in 271, seventeen under par. This "record" for four rounds would be matched thirty years later by Jack Nicklaus, who set the competitive Masters standard in 1965; his official mark of 271 was equalled by Raymond Floyd in winning the 1976 Masters.*

*A blistering 63 by Nick Price in the third round in 1986 set the tournament record, breaking the old mark of 64 first set by Lloyd Mangrum in 1940; Price's mark stood for ten years before his good friend, Greg Norman, matched it in the first round in 1996. Neither man won.*

# JACK NICKLAUS

LEFT

*A golden era in Masters history opened in 1959 with the arrival of a stocky amateur named Jack Nicklaus*

BOTTOM LEFT

*Nicklaus signs an autograph in 1965 after firing a tournament record 271 while his father, Charlie Nicklaus, shares the moment.*

BOTTOM RIGHT

*Jack's booming cannon shots were a natural for the wide open spaces at the Augusta National, but it was his putting and mental approach that brought him six green jackets.*

TOP

*A slimmed-down Jack Nicklaus, his power undiminished, went after his fourth green coat in 1972, and got it despite closing rounds of 73-74; no one in the field could mount a serious challenge.*

BOTTOM

*The magical finish in 1986 will be remembered as long as the Masters is played, with Nicklaus overtaking first Watson, then Ballesteros, and finally Kite and Norman at the end, accompanied by Jack Jr., his caddie, and all culminating with this walk up the hill from the last green, father and son linked in unspoken affection.*

*Tom Watson, with the face of Tom Sawyer and the heart of Jesse James, took part in two epic duels in 1977 with rival Jack Nicklaus, including the one at the Masters which Watson won after Jack closed with 66 and Tom with 67.*

*Tom Watson strides confidently from the thirteenth green in 1981, the year he won his second Masters, holding off the challenges of Jack Nicklaus, Johnny Miller, and Greg Norman. Below, the master of the short game escapes from yet another bunker.*

# GARY PLAYER

LEFT

*Never more dangerous than when cornered, Gary Player escaped time and time again from desperate spots. Here the South African, clad all in black as was his custom in those days, contemplates another miracle shot during his march to victory in 1974.*

OPPOSITE PAGE

*Gary Player strides up the eighteenth, to finish off a run of seven birdies over the final ten holes and a score of 64 in 1978. He receives kisses from his daughter and son, after being helped into his third green jacket by defender Tom Watson, one of three who failed by a stroke to catch Gary that year.*

*Jack Nicklaus does the honors, helping Arnold Palmer into his green jacket in 1964, the year Palmer became the first to win four Masters. Arnie finished six strokes ahead of Dave Marr and Nicklaus, who would himself win the next two Masters.*

*A gallant but ill-starred Ed Sneed stares anxiously at his ball as it hangs on the edge of the cup but fails to drop at the last hole of the 1979 Masters, sending him into a playoff with Tom Watson and eventual winner, Fuzzy Zoeller.*

*A young Ray Floyd, at right, tees off in one of his first Masters. In the photo below, Floyd chips close during his runaway victory in 1976 in which he tied the tournament record of 271, set by Jack Nicklaus in 1965. Floyd shot 65 in the first round, and led all four rounds, finishing eight strokes ahead of runnerup Ben Crenshaw.*

*Jumbo Ozaki, Japan's outstanding internationalist, applies serious body English to a long putt. Ozaki first played in the Masters in 1972 and has been a big favorite on the Augusta National course where his booming tee shots often put him in contention.*

*Seve Ballesteros, the master of escape from any place he can reach, has won two Masters, and very nearly three others, despite visits to bunkers, the flower beds at thirteen (opposite, top), the forests at ten, and the grandstands at eighteen (opposite, below).*

*Bernhard Langer in 1985 became only the third foreigner, after Gary Player and Seve Ballesteros, to win the Masters, but not the last, as everyone has seen. Langer won again in 1993 when his bold eagle at thirteen on the final day widened the lead over Chip Beck to three strokes, a lead that was not challenged; he shared the honors with his young daughter.*

*After a glorious seven-iron from the fairway bunker at eighteen, Sandy Lyle lined up this ten-footer down the hill and calmly stroked it in to claim victory in 1988 in another of those wild Sunday finishes; he edged Mark Calcavecchia by one stroke.*

*One of the most startling days in Masters history began Sunday, April 14, 1996, with Greg Norman leading Nick Faldo, with whom he was paired, by six strokes, and ended with Faldo the winner by five, having gained an astonishing eleven strokes in that final round. The scores were 67 and 78. An appreciative gallery awaits the start, above, and, at right, Faldo caddie Fanny Sunnesson is caught between winner and loser at the end.*

*Faldo became the sixth man, after Demaret, Snead, Palmer, Nicklaus, and Player, to win three Masters, and only the second to win consecutive titles; Nicklaus is the other.*

# DRAMATIC FINISHES

THERE HAVE BEEN SO MANY close and dramatic finishes in the Masters, we have almost come to expect them every year. The design of the golf course, with its slick, undulating greens and its risk vs. reward holes on the inward nine, together with the increasingly deep pool of talent in the game, seem to encourage the kind of gang finishes we have seen in recent years, with no apparent end in sight. In 1960, in response to a letter from Howard Gill, the publisher of *Golf Digest*, Bob Jones listed his choices of the most dramatic finishes up to that time. With his comments, Jones' choices were:

1935 — The most dramatic, which would be the choice of everyone, was that provided by Gene Sarazen in the second Masters when he holed the double eagle at the fifteenth hole in the final round.

1942 — The playoff in which Byron Nelson picked up six strokes in eleven holes and defeated Ben Hogan, 69 to 70. This had long remained in my mind as one of the most magnificent golfing contests I have ever witnessed.

1959 — Art Wall's closing 66 to beat Cary Middlecoff by one stroke and Arnold Palmer by two. Any time a competitor can finish with five birdies in the last six holes, as Art Wall did, he can be said to have provided his share of drama.

1949 — In a similar vein was Sam Snead's brilliant comeback when he played the last two rounds in matching 67s after being far back at the end of two rounds.

Since 1960, any number of Masters finishes might be added to Bob Jones' list. These six come readily to mind:

1960 — Arnold Palmer secured his claim on the affections of America's golf fans when he came to the seventeenth on the final day trailing Ken Venturi by one, and proceeded to birdie the last two holes to win by a stroke and capture his second Masters.

1975 — Despite closing rounds of 65-66 by Johnny Miller and a great duel with Miller and Tom Weiskopf on the back nine, Jack Nicklaus closed with 68 to finish at 276, one stroke in front of his rivals. Both missed birdie tries at the last which would have forced a playoff; it was Weiskopf's fourth near miss.

1978 — Gary Player started the final round seven strokes back of the leader, fired seven birdies in the last ten holes on his way to a 64 and edged defending champ Tom Watson, Hubert Green, and Rod Funseth by a stroke.

1986 — Jack Nicklaus, at the age of forty-six, was four strokes behind with four to play and finished 3-2-3-4 for 30 on the back to beat Tom Kite and Greg

TOP

*In 1975, in one of the Masters Tournament's more exciting finishes, Tom Weiskopf came this close to tying Jack Nicklaus, which would have forced a playoff.*

BOTTOM

*Nicklaus takes the seat of honor at the awards ceremony, having turned back the challenges of both Weiskopf, on left, and Johnny Miller, center.*

# DRAMATIC FINISHES (CONTINUED)

Norman — each of whom had a chance to tie at the last — by a single stroke. The green jacket was Jack's sixth, a record not likely to be matched.

1987 — The storybook finish by Larry Mize, who holed a most dramatic birdie chip at the eleventh, to beat Greg Norman in a playoff (described more fully elsewhere).

1989 — In some of the worst weather in Masters history, Nick Faldo survived a third-round 77 and a wild chase among six players in the final round with a closing 65, then holed a monster putt for birdie at the eleventh in the fading twilight to win a playoff with Scott Hoch, who had himself missed a short one at ten that would have ended things.

*Jack Nicklaus knew the clincher when he had it, and this long birdie putt at seventeen, which helped him to a closing 65, climaxed a dramatic come-from-behind victory over Greg Norman and Tom Kite in 1986.*

EXIT